RESEARCH INTO TEACHING METHODS IN HIGHER EDUCATION
MAINLY IN BRITISH UNIVERSITIES
Third edition

by

RUTH M. BEARD M.Sc. M.A. Ph.D.

and

DONALD A. BLIGH B.A.

Society for Research into Higher Education Ltd
20 Gower Street, London WC1E 6DP

July 1971

Dr. Ruth Beard is the holder of two degrees in Mathematics and two in Education. She has taught in grammar schools, a comprehensive school, a college of education and two University Institutes of Education. Dr. Beard is currently Senior Lecturer in Higher Education and is in charge of the University Teaching Methods Unit, University of London Institute of Education. The Leverhulme Trust financed the Unit between 1965 and 1968 and is supporting an investigation into objectives in teaching which began late in 1968.

After training as a teacher, Donald Bligh took degrees in geography at Leeds, and philosophy and psychology at Birkbeck College, London. Before joining the University Teaching Methods Unit, he taught in Art and Technical Colleges, Adult Education and a Polytechnic. He has conducted research into the effectiveness of lectures and other teaching methods in Higher Education.

First published September 1967
Second edition September 1968
Third edition July 1971

Cover design

by

JENNIE WEBB

FOREWORD

The first edition of this monograph which appeared in September 1967 sold out in eight months. Because there were already sixty additional references which justified one new section and several substantial amplifications of existing sections, it was followed by a second edition, rather than a reprint, in September 1968. Although this also sold quickly, heavy commitments have not permitted me until now to write a third edition; but, since they have continued to sell steadily, reprints of the second edition were evidently still useful.

Despite the accumulation of many new references in the intervening two and a half years, section headings have required little alteration. Only one new section has been added, 'Programmed Learning', although others have been amplified considerably. My prediction in 1968 that simulation systems would be developed rapidly proved correct, but the number of experiments in this field has been small. The sections in which experimental work has been most abundant are those dealing with audio-visual aids, including programmed learning.

On this occasion I have invited my colleague, Donald Bligh, to share in the labour of searching journals and rewriting the text. He has been responsible for substantial additions and alterations to the section on 'Recall and Retention of Information' and for many additions and some alterations in the section on 'Evaluation of Students, Teachers and Teaching Methods'. We feel sure that we have missed some interesting articles, for the number of journals which print contributions on research into teaching and learning has increased so greatly. We should be very grateful to readers if they will draw our attention to omissions.

The extensive work, mentioned in 1968, on the specification of objectives and related methods in teaching and evaluation, is not yet published and must therefore be discussed in the fourth edition. This, we hope, will appear within less than another two and a half years.

RMB

CONTENTS

INTRODUCTION

During a course for new lecturers in the sciences at the University of London Institute of Education in 1968 a number of small group discussions were held on methods of teaching and on aspects of learning and relevant findings in research. The majority of the participants enjoyed the discussions and found them profitable; but one group leader, a psychologist, reported as follows of discussions in a group drawn from various departments: 'It was striking to find that university graduates, with sometimes years of research experience, were unable to apply to the problems of teaching the same methods of scientific inquiry they would, presumably, use in their own discipline: statement of problem, collection of observations, statement of hypothesis, test of hypothesis by experimentation including appropriate controls'. The same group leader reported of a further session of discussion '... the discussion seemed to go very little way towards encouraging a scientific approach to teaching: statement of aims, experiments in teaching method, evaluation of teaching and of student learning. Even the paucity of factual data on these was not appreciated.'

Perhaps scientists whose subjects have a sound theoretical foundation do not feel at home with a subject which lacks a theory. For, not only is there no theory of teaching to turn to when problems arise, but theories of learning are too numerous and too little concerned with human learning to provide a framework for action. Teachers cannot design courses taking into account the numerous variables in learning and personal interactions, but must introduce innovations largely on the basis of induction from their observations. Nevertheless, we should expect that scientists, if not other university teachers, would appreciate the need to experiment to determine the effectiveness of innovations introduced in teaching.

Reports from other groups suggested that this one may have been somewhat exceptional, but their non-scientific attitude to teaching was repeated in an appreciable minority of participants in the course. On the whole such an attitude was less prevalent among biologists, doctors, dentists, psychologists and specialists in education, all of whom are accustomed to experimenting with variable, living organisms, than among mathematicians, physicists, chemists and engineers who handle or observe more predictable inanimate materials and symbols. What differences there are probably arise from basic differences in experience, some of the physical scientists considering experiments non-scientific if the conclusions can be stated only in terms of probabilities. Since, in addition, by no means all educational experiments are rigorously designed, some scientists may tend to reject the results wholly. But, in doing so, they discard the few sound beginnings in scientific method which have so far been made in the educational field and revert to attitudes and subjective judgements appropriate to a pre-scientific era. The remedies lie in more widespread use of good designs in educational experiments as well as appreciation on the part of teachers that results of experiments which are stated only in terms of probabilities may yet have value in guiding policies or in the selection of teaching methods.

Until comparatively recently all changes in university teaching were due to outstanding innovators in the universities or followed on recommendations of committees and professional bodies. Few of these have been directly influenced by findings in the psychology of learning or experiments into the effectiveness of teaching methods but were based almost exclusively on teachers' views as to how the subject should develop, their experience of learning and teaching and knowledge of methods used elsewhere. The findings of psychologists are unlikely to supersede such recommendations by experts but should contribute to them increasingly. Since in the case of preparing programmed books, or setting up television as an aid to teaching, for example, expenditure of time or money may be considerable, there has been a fairly large number of experiments to determine their value as compared with traditional teaching. It is also the psychologists, and lecturers who have taken part in teaching experiments, who have made us aware that some innovations in teaching prove to be stimulating for a time, like fashions, but may soon produce no more response than their predecessors. Consequently any conscientious attempt to devise ways of teaching which are essentially more effective must involve the teacher in specifying his aims, devising methods to achieve them and undertaking, or allowing, an evaluation of their success in terms of students' achievements and attitudes over a period of time.

The experimental work mentioned in the ensuing pages is restricted to that in British higher education, mainly in universities, to the end of 1970. Two surveys already exist of American work (Eckert and Neale 1965; McKeachie, 1966), but these will be referred to only where the contributions of research workers in America greatly exceed those from British sources.

AIMS AND OBJECTIVES

In teaching any subject, clarification of aims is essential for two main reasons: firstly, in the majority of subjects there are many possible objectives so that, if time and resources are not to be wasted, a choice must be made between them; secondly, it is only possible to determine whether teaching and learning have been effective if it is first decided what they should achieve. Aims need to be defined at a number of different levels. The ultimate goals of a course, such as acquisition of professional competence and appropriate attitudes, must be decided by specialists in the field from their combined knowledge of subject matter and social demands on the profession; but, once these are settled, many intermediate goals are needed both as a guide in teaching and to provide students with direction in studying and a sense of achievement as each goal is attained.

It is perhaps hardly surprising that very few attempts have been made to assess the effects of whole courses, for it is a considerable and lengthy undertaking. There are no British studies of the kind, but inevitably there is some feedback into the universities as to the adequacy of students' training when they take up their professions. It is sometimes suggested, for example, that industry needs scientists with a more general scientific training to enable them to adjust to inevitable changes in technology with greater flexibility, and many general practitioners are critical of medical training as a preparation for their profession. To some extent this may reflect the different attitudes of theoretical and applied scientists. The theoretician tends to remain in the university and may be poorly informed about practical applications of his subject, whereas the practical scientist tends to disregard theory except in so far as it is immediately useful. Both attitudes raise problems for students. Engineering students, for example, complain when taught by mathematicians who cannot show how to apply their mathematical knowledge whereas, if taught without a sound theoretical basis by men from industry, their knowledge cannot be readily adapted to changing conditions. The theoretician will most probably be satisfied with evidence that the student has sufficient understanding to explain or reorganize what he has learned and to make inferences, generalizations and predictions from it; but all this demonstrates is that he has a capacity to organize his knowledge mentally; it provides no evidence of ability to apply knowledge. The practical scientist needs to be taught principles and applications together and this objective can probably only be attained by closer co-operation between teachers from different fields.

Recent reports confirm industry's need for scientists who have studied broadly based courses. Both the Swann (1968) and the McCarthy Reports (1968) conclude that, in future, only 40 per cent of scientists will require highly specialized scientific knowledge and recommend that the majority of students should take a two year course in sciences which provides a knowledge of basic principles. An alternative approach to broadening science curricula is already in operation in Sussex (Daiches, 1964). In Manchester a new course is designed to give insight into the role of science in relation to politics, economics, industry, and philosophy while offering a broad coverage of physics and chemistry with some engineering and computer programming (Jevons, 1970). Students from this course have proved highly marketable, many going straight into industry. A new M.Sc. course in the same department requires more extended studies of social issues relating to the sciences. Heywood (1969) outlines the B.Sc course in engineering at Bath which achieves breadth by requiring students to study a unified course initially before proceeding to engineering design and a laboratory course together with a language or social study; in addition students choose subjects from a number of electives aimed at continuing a broad education.

New courses to meet demands for greater flexibility have also been introduced in sciences in the University of London (Burge, 1968; Jones, 1969) and in the department of physics at the University of Surrey (Elton, 1968; Elton et al., 1970). In a B.Ed. course integrated studies linking subject areas are used with a view to avoiding the rigidity of subject divisions (Gill, 1970). London allows students to select from nine to twelve approved 'course units', where a 'course unit' represents 'one third of the total work load which every student who is capable of obtaining a degree at all should be able to manage' in a year. A two-subject degree may, therefore, be taken with a number of different weightings between the subjects; currently, there are four weightings for combined courses in physics and mathematics. Degree courses attractive to employers are encouraged; thus, a physicist who wishes to apply his knowledge in biophysics may take some units in biology or biochemistry, a biochemist interested in macromolecular structure may take a course in computer programming, etc. In the latter course, there are a and β alternatives in each year, with some overlap between the years, so allowing a student to study more difficult courses in topics he is good at. A system of credits is based on time spent on a course together with its difficulty level.

Thus these courses, like those at Keele and Sussex, are in line with recommendations of the Robbins Report that a greater proportion of undergraduates should receive a broader education and that, wherever possible, the decision between special and general courses should be deferred to the end of the first year.

What 'assessment' of courses there is, in British Schools, consists in inviting students to express criticisms or to make suggestions during staff-student conferences or by way of questionnaires. The use of questionnaires is becoming more common in London's Medical Schools (Beard, 1967 b) and an opinion poll on lectures, prepared by dental students, has been reported in a supplement to their School journal (Students' Society Committee, 1966).

If asked to define their aims university teachers usually include general aims such as encouragement of 'scientific attitude', capacity for critical thinking, independence on the part of students, and so on. Evidently what these teachers hope to achieve is transfer of attitudes and skills developed in their own field to other situations in life; but studies in America suggest that this may rarely be achieved. The only one of these studies recorded in a partly British journal tested for changes in political knowledge, participation and values resulting from courses mainly in social sciences, but there was little evidence of any impact in these respects (McClintock and Turner, 1962).

In two inquiries into the aims and choice of teaching methods among 21 teachers in a department of psychiatry, Walton and Drewery found widely different aims (Walton and Drewery, 1964 and 1966). It is true that every teacher stated as one of his objectives the provision of systematic information, but this was the exclusive goal of three of them, six others taught with a psycho-dynamic orientation, seven shared these goals but also aimed to teach behavioural science while the remaining five aimed, in addition, to modify the behaviour of students. Hospital staff lecturers and teachers with an unidimensional subject orientation tended to have aims of the first two, the differences between these groups being significant. Aims were less clearly related to choice of teaching methods than to the teacher's speciality, but those most in favour of group work emphasized teaching for students' self-knowledge and viewing patients in the family context.

The revelation of such a diversity of aims within one department stresses the need to state overall objectives of a course, and suggests that considerable discussion might be needed before the introduction of major changes requiring all members of staff to accept aims wider than provision of information. Indeed, discussion would probably show that members of staff had different interpretations of 'systematic information'; or they might disagree as to methods of determining whether this objective had been attained. Similar comments apply to most of the objectives we quote below except those spelled out in detail for programmed courses.

Differences in aims may also be expected between teachers of different university subjects. In a pilot inquiry into the use of small group discussion in departments of mathematics, electrical engineering and biology in London University (Beard, 1967 a), lecturers in any one subject had many different aims in using discussion but there was also some differentiation between subjects. The aim mentioned most frequently by mathematicians and engineers was to discover and to discuss students' difficulties; mathematicians mentioned this 13 times, engineers 10 times. The biologists showed a different emphasis giving as their most frequent aims: to encourage critical thinking, to look afresh at familiar problems (eight times), to explore other subject matter or an individual topic (eight times) and to encourage reading (five times). Some of the engineers also mentioned increase of activity on the part of the student with moderate frequency: to encourage active participation (five times), to stimulate students into thinking and reading (five times) and to develop ability to speak fluently or to make verbal reports (five times). The table shows an analysis of aims for each subject into three categories: provision of aid to students in difficulties, stimulating some kind of independent activity, or 'other'. The last category includes such aims as: 'to reduce routine lecturing', 'to give opportunity to investigate in depth aspects of a course which is brief and therefore shallow', 'to provide more intimate and personal staff-student contact' and so on.

Aim	Mathematics	Electrical Engineering	Biology
To aid students	28	25	15
To encourage independent activity	10	23	28
Other	9	8	5

The clear difference in emphasis, on giving assistance or encouraging independent activity, raises questions which cannot yet be answered with any certainty. For instance: does difference in subject matter wholly account for it? Mathematicians might argue that independent activity and critical thinking were essential to even modest success in their subject so that removal of difficulties automatically gives rise to both. In biology, however, a weak student may be satisfied if he reads uncritically and reports information directly from a textbook; he is not brought face to face with his inadequacies as a weak student in mathematics is when he fails to solve problems. In addition, living things differ in their behaviour on different occasions, so a biologist must be trained to be critical of a single experiment or of a few experiments. Apart from these differences in subject matter, aims are likely to differ with the age and seniority of the students. In mathematics, most discussion groups were held with first-year students; in biology, second-year students were best represented but group discussions for third year and postgraduate students were also more numerous than in mathematics. At higher levels we should expect students to be led increasingly to independent activity. A third possible cause of difference in aims between teachers in these two subjects may be the work of Abercrombie, whose book <u>The Anatomy of Judgment</u> is based on work in a biology department and shows the use of group discussion in promoting critical thinking (Abercrombie, 1965). It is likely that this is better known in biology departments although it seems reasonably certain that her findings have wider application.

Not only are different objectives required in different subjects, or entertained by different teachers, but students too attend universities with a diversity of expectations. In a factorial study in Australia (Katz and Katz, 1968) three clusters of objectives were identified, the first emphasizing general and liberalizing effects desired from a university education, the second concerned with development of expertise in a special field and the third with training for a specific vocation.

Intermediate aims of various kinds are of great importance in giving direction to learning and in promoting confidence and motivation by their successive achievement. This is one aspect in which the contributions of psychologists and others designing objective tests or writing programmed books are so valuable, for they break down the ultimate aims of a course into many intermediate objectives. A few examples will serve to show the value both to a student who wishes to learn, or to revise, independently and to the teacher. In the first place, two aims provided by Mr. E.A.H. Martin (Department of Botany, Glasgow University) are broken down in this way:

A. Aim: 'To understand the Hardy-Weinberg Law'

> Objectives: 1. The student will be able to give a written definition of the law.
>
> 2. The student will be able to derive the Hardy-Weinberg formula.
>
> 3. The student will be able to list four conditions described in a population before the gene frequencies given by the formula will be valid.

B. Aim: 'To understand sex-linked inheritance'

> Objectives: 1. Given several family trees, the student will be able to select those in which there is a sex-linked trait.
>
> 2. The student will be able to forecast the percentage of affected individuals of a mating, given the genotype of the parents.

It is possible that if the reader teaches biology he has now remarked that the objectives listed above are more or less those which he would in any case follow and that there is, therefore, no particular value in outlining what is so obvious. If so, it may serve a useful purpose to list a second set of objectives broken down in a similar fashion, this time in electrical engineering (provided by Mr. J.B. Thomas, Brunel University).

<u>Aim</u>: 'To understand magnetohydrodynamic power generation (MHD)'

<u>Objectives</u>: 1. To give a brief but accurate account, in descriptive terms of the basic physical principles of MHD generation.

2. To draw a sketch which illustrates unambiguously the reasons for the MHD power generation, in terms of the movement of hot ionised gases through a magnetic field, etc.

3. To list the practical problems arising from the high temperature required for MHD generation.

4. To list, compare and contrast, the advantages and disadvantages of the open and closed cycles for MHD generation.

5. To discuss the forecast of the economics of MHD generation in terms of :-
   5.1. capital expenditure and running costs of MHD plant,
   5.2. 'topping up' conventional steam plant.

Objectives for a complete course have been outlined in this way by B.J. Hill (1969) who reports that

(i)   such statements of objectives are much more informative to students and to other teachers than the conventional form of syllabus statement,

(ii) the explicit statement of objectives and the classification of lecture material helps to ensure that the material is appropriate to the lectures and that the correct emphasis is given to it,

(iii) the assessment procedures can be made to test for the attainment of the specific objectives of the course.

In addition to the provision of intermediate objectives such as these, short term objectives play an influential part in certain kinds of learning and teaching. In programmed learning the short term objective of the learner is to give the correct answer to the next frame; in following a logical argument the student may try to decide the next step before it is spoken or written; and, in learning from tapes or slides, the immediate objective may be to give a correct answer to the next question. In every case it is crucial that the answer should be given almost at once so that a correct response is reinforced and a wrong one immediately corrected. Where the objective in teaching is learning of information or understanding and application of principles short term objectives of this kind can add considerably to the efficiency of learning.

In certain kinds of learning there is no need to supply an answer since checks are intrinsic; when learning to type, or in rote-learning vocabulary, for example, the learner knows at once that he has made a mistake and what to do to correct it. In such a case learning is likely to proceed rapidly; but in many kinds of higher learning students require to be told whether they are right or wrong and this must happen before learning can proceed further. It is in such tasks that it is important to provide students with fairly rapid feed-back on their success – by providing questions and lists of answers, outlines of solutions etc., or by making comments on exercises – since in this way they are motivated to learn more rapidly. Experiments have been described, even with postgraduates, in which questions requiring written answers were introduced during a lecture and immediately corrected, which resulted in greater enthusiasm and markedly more rapid and effective learning (Beard, 1967 a).

A comprehensive approach to defining objectives in a course, using all these methods, as appropriate, has been made in an Art College (Burke, 1967; Piper, 1967), which employed an occupational psychologist. Analysis of the work of designers led to discarding the traditional subject-based course in favour of one aimed to develop abilities in solving design problems, to provide a knowledge of the context in which designers work and to enable students to learn to establish relationships with management. The aims of the course are described, there-fore, in operational terms, showing what students should become capable of doing at various stages. These aims and the related performance requirements are set out in extensive charts which serve as a 'syllabus' and 'timetable' both to staff and students. The course is associated with a different attitude to students' learning. From the beginning, students are asked to think about problems, and teaching staff cease to give factual information but guide students to use their own expertise and to obtain necessary information in the course of solving problems.

Staff of the University Teaching Methods Unit of London University Institute of Education are currently engaged in working with university teachers to define objectives in teaching and to relate these to methods in teaching and assessment. Early stages of this work are described by Beard (1970). Subjects at present under consideration are physics, dentistry, architecture and chemistry; in addition schemes of this kind are being developed for training in General Practice in medicine, for student teachers of biology, and in physiotherapy. An investiga-tion into teachers' objectives in setting examinations in biochemistry is soon to be published (Beard and Pole, 1971).

Comprehensive and systematic analysis of objectives, evaluation and teaching methods is, of course, employed by writers of programmed texts and occupa-tional psychologists. Indeed it is this which is advocated as an essential procedure by all educational technologists. Extension of the method to higher education is very recent but it is now recommended as a step in developing more relevant and effective courses (Eraut, 1970; MacKenzie et al., 1970). A brief reconsideration of objectives is sometimes sufficient to reorient teachers if this allows them to question their objectives and procedures in relation to the purposes of higher education, the needs of students and the structure of subject matter and, possibly, professional requirements. Elton (1970) recommends a fundamental re-examination of this kind to mathematicians who teach courses to scientists and engineers. Dudley (1970) has made a modest beginning in clinical medicine.

An extensive inquiry into objectives in teaching psychology to student teachers has been conducted in the colleges of education of the Birmingham University Institute of Education (Stones and Anderson, 1970). Tutors and students of the colleges, and school teachers were asked to rate objectives which had been

collected from relevant literature or from teachers' statements. Close agreement was found between the three groups who all rated very highly: willingness
to vary teaching methods and to meet the needs of individuals, adaptability to a
variety of teaching situations; ability to distinguish between rote and meaningful
learning; ability to identify and help failing children, that the teacher should be
a leader in learning situations rather than a source of information, that she
should be able to prepare effective instructional procedures in teaching reading,
that she should be free from dogmatic precepts and emotional thinking, able to
outline factors influencing emotional development in children or the most
important social influences in learning and able to assess the influence of play in
children's development. Since, however, no fundamental reappraisal of the
purpose of teaching psychology to student teachers was undertaken, this is
limited to an interesting descriptive study of what is currently accepted. It is
not an attempt to re-examine and thus to improve practice.

Methods of occupational psychologists have also been used by designers and
architects (Broadbent, 1968; Darke, 1968) and by physicists in planning a
lecture course and in preparing a guide to the postgraduate education of
physicists. Williams and Wooding (1967, 1968) used net-work analyses to set
out in diagrams the activities involved in a lecture programme and in planning
a research. This involved analysis of the activities involved, showing the order
of events and the relationships between the activities; drawing the net-work
entailed and defining the objective of the programme, setting out the successive
activities to attain the objective and making estimates of the time required for
the completion of each activity. This kind of presentation permits greater
generalization of the material and displays omissions or redundancies. Two
net-works, in a series of six, show how each task is attempted (figures 1 and 2).
But although this approach will lead to greater efficiency it will not, of course,
help to overcome the complaints concerning some Ph.Ds, reported by the
Institute of Physics (1960), that they lack scientific originality, a good theoretical
background in physics or flexibility and adaptability in thinking.

A different approach is used by Doughty (1970) who explores relationships
between topics by means of a matrix, so identifying fairly independent concept
areas and the best order in which to present them in teaching biomedical
subjects.

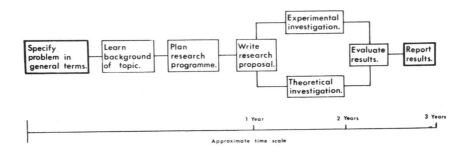

Figure 1.   Overall plan of research project.

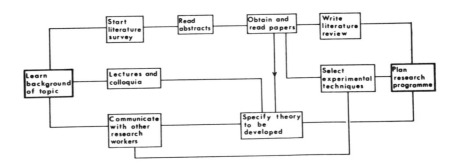

Figure 2.   Activities involved in learning the background of a subject.

ECONOMY AND EFFICIENCY

Under this heading we shall consider experiments in which one important objective was to reduce time occupied in teaching by increase in class size, absence of the teacher for part of the time, or by reorganization of teaching. But it is of interest that economists are now beginning to investigate efficiency and productivity of university education (Blaug, 1968).

Only two experiments described in British journals are specifically concerned with class size: de Cecco (1964) assigned 682 students randomly to three kinds of groups, two large experimental ones consisting of 97 and 127 subjects, six small experimental groups ranging in size from 18 to 34 subjects and 10 small control groups ranging from 22 to 35. All courses in the experimental groups followed the same outline including major assignments, instructional materials and a common grading system but, in the control group, instructors proceeded as normal, selecting their own materials and creating their own assignments. In the four tests given subsequently, no significant differences were found in acquisition of information or understanding but the students greatly preferred smaller groups.

Cottrell (1962) used groups of three, 12 and 24 members in an attempt to discover how large a discussion group could be in physical chemistry without loss of efficiency. A short answer–paper was set on matter of fact and simple problems following weekly discussions throughout one term. Groups as large as 24 proved unpopular and inefficient but the success ratio (calculated by dividing each student's score by his mean marks in class examinations in chemistry the previous year) was consistently higher for the groups of 12.

Extensive studies on the class size made in the United States, having conflicting results, are reported by McKeachie (1966) who concludes that the importance of size depends on educational goals: 'In general, large classes are simply not as effective as small classes for retention, critical thinking and attitude change'.

Learning in small groups may also be more effective than individual activities. Tubbs (1968) reports that he works with groups of about eight students to help them to learn more about experimentation. A problem is outlined by the tutor, suggestions are invited from students and these are discussed in some detail. The students then choose apparatus and spend three or four hours in making measurements, each in a different way. Finally they discuss reasons for differences in their results and sources of experimental error. The method proves economical of staff time and, usually, of apparatus. Tubbs considers that first year students can usefully spend up to twenty per cent of laboratory time in this way. However, there is no experimental evaluation of the method.

Programmed learning is another recent development which offers the tutor an opportunity to reduce instruction time. A series of experiments to compare programmed learning in science with conventional teaching, at the same time using only one trained instructor where formerly two were employed, has been made very successfully in the Navy (Stavert and Wingate, 1966). 10 pairs of classes were taught by conventional methods or by programmed learning in basic electronics, basic radio and in associated laboratory work. While one group followed the programme and illustrative films with the aid of a junior technician, the other received conventional teaching from an Instruction Officer. Since in every case results from programmed learning equalled or excelled those of conventional teaching it was clearly possible and indeed even beneficial, to cut instruction time by half. Failure rates were 14 per cent and three per cent less and final average marks were 62 in each case as compared with 55 and 54, in electronics and radio respectively. In addition time taken by programmed learning in radio was 25 per cent less, on average, than that for conventional instruction. Experiments in the RAF confirm that, when used over a period of weeks, students using programmed learning took considerably less time, particularly in the case of those using a programme reduced to essentials, but achieved results similar to those of apprentices studying by conventional methods (Wallis et al., 1966). More recently this has been confirmed in a course for medical science personnel who attempted programmes having five differing amounts of redundancy (Valverdi and Morgan, 1970); it was the leanest programme which proved most economical and efficient. Statistics programmes seem to be less successful, however. J.R. Hartley (1968) reports a study with 138 university students in which a programme exerted greater control over students' work habits and led to a higher overall mean mark on test of retention, application and transfer; but 47 per cent of the students completed less than three quarters of the programme compared with only 19 per cent of the control group who failed to read the book. Thus in this case the programme achieved a better result at the expense of greater effort which was unacceptable to many students; but the possibility of cutting the programme is not discussed.

In industry, Romiszowski (1962) reports that about half the large industrial firms now use programmed learning. Education officers find that it results in better retention, faster learning and flexibility in teaching since it can proceed without supervision. Adult students find programmed learning less embarrassing than class teaching since they do not need to admit ignorance in public. In addition, the results are continuously assessable and controllable.

Criticisms are often made of experiments in programmed learning on account of their brevity, inadequate testing of the programme or poor quality of teaching compared with the programmed learning course. Almost all of the experiments quoted in this article, however, were of fairly long duration, covering whole courses in a number of cases; the programmes were carefully tested and teaching, compared with the programmes, was of a high or unusually high standard, based on the content of the programmes themselves.

It may be that findings in the Forces and in industry are irrelevant at university level but only experiments with carefully prepared programmes can show whether this is so. However, Moore (1967) found in an experiment with university students that group teaching by a method of pacing, setting a time limit for each frame, resulted in a considerably better speed for slow workers. Times for the machine group were of the order of 30 per cent less than that of slower workers using self-paced books. This saving was effected without significantly affecting the test scores. Biran and Pickering (1968) found that 'unscrambling' a branching programme in genetics and presenting it in linear form decreased learning time without affecting gain in scores. Teather (1968) in listing programmes for teaching biology, notes the saving in time and the possibility of using programmes for experiments with alternative teaching sequences.

Comparisons of different conventional methods of teaching show that the lecture is more economical of time than other methods if each is used independently.

Joyce and Weatherall (1957), in comparing different methods of teaching (lectures, discussion groups, practical classes and unsupervised reading) in a carefully designed experiment, concluded that lecturing was the most efficient method of teaching since it used least of the students' and staff's time: 'For tutors the size of classes is relevant to the economics of teaching, and the figures amount to 0.05 hours per session per student for lectures (assuming an audience of 60); 0.3 hours per session per student for discussion groups of 12 students, and 0.33 hours per session per student for practical classes on the same scale.... these estimates are probably reliable enough to emphasize the economy, both to students and staff of lecturing compared with practical classes and discussion groups....'. But they commented that a simple comparison of the four methods might not have shown all of them to the best advantage: for example, discussion groups might have been more efficient when used to develop material already presented by other methods.

In a second experiment (1959) they used a more complex, but equally carefully chosen design, to compare methods in which the contribution of teachers' time was small with others in which the teachers were more fully involved. 62 preclinical students were taught by four initial lectures and either three demonstrations or three practical classes in conjunction with either three conventional seminars or three discussion meetings initiated by playing back recorded material. Gain in knowledge did not differ significantly from one group to another, but demonstrations were much more economical of time than practical classes for teachers, technicians and students (practicals taking about 20 per cent more time for students and teachers); discussion required less time of teachers than seminars, but the corresponding difference for students was slight.

MacManaway (1968) confirmed the efficiency of lectures in comparing recall of lecture material and the same material learned by reading lecture scripts and note-taking. Reading and note-taking took considerably longer, but, in a test given a week later, students in both groups did about equally well. A third group who attended the lecture and made notes subsequently took still more time but did no better.

One experiment, however, shows that combination of methods, using some discussion but no lectures, may be highly efficient. To Erskine and Tomkin (1963), reduction of time spent on a course was a major consideration. They substituted two periods of group discussion for nine lectures during a period of three weeks spent in studying the anatomy of the pelvis. Following an introductory demonstration using specially prepared specimens and models, practical work was done in the usual way, but with access to practical materials at any time during the day and with informal demonstrations on request. The discussion groups were introduced at the ends of the second and third weeks. On each occasion lists were displayed which drew attention to a number of points in the course of practical work, and a central theme was agreed on for discussion between the four instructors in order to organize the facts into a pattern. Consequently the students arrived well prepared at the discussions, in which there was a free exchange of views resulting in synthesis at the end of each section.

The experiment was not a controlled one in which parallel groups were treated differently, but an attempt was made to assess its success by comparing results of students in two successive years, and each group of students with themselves in anatomy of the pelvis and of the thorax. Objective tests, essays and oral examinations were all used in the assessment. It appeared reasonably clear that there was no loss of information as a result of the change in method, but rather the contrary, and students who attended discussion groups were far more successful in oral examinations. But the chief gain was of seven hours time in the case of each student and one hour to each member of staff.

In this last experiment we have evidence not only of reduction in time spent but also of better recall of recently learned material. Experiments with pro-grammed learning have also resulted in gains in both these respects, but at present there are few programmes suited to university work. However, where recall, or retention, is as good as that for lectures or other methods depending on the presence of teachers, the gain in teaching time is obvious. Similar gains may be made with more relevant or better planned activities using audio-visual techniques. In an Australian 'experiment' (Collard et al., 1969) in teaching chemistry, university students who constructed organic molecules in plastic and sketched completed models, instead of merely studying from text-books and copying diagrams, showed a marked improvement in under-standing of three-dimensional aspects of molecular structure. And in medical teaching in Glasgow, where the ratio of staff to students is low, a collection of programmed tape-slide presentations enables students to work independently at their own speed (Harden et al., 1969); the experimental group using this technique did significantly better than the control group who followed a conven-tional course, the three overseas students rising from the lower to the upper half of the class as a whole. Lewinson (1970) reports self-testing devices in clinical medicine using a quizz board displaying pictures, slides or X-rays together with questions as to diagnosis etc. A lift-up card displays answers and a folder supplies references. The advantage of the method is that it can be used during spare intervals and a third of the students say that they find it valuable.

Activities and information designed to enable students to make better use of facilities or to benefit from a course also add to efficiency. A one-week, pre-college maths. workshop organized by Taylor and Hanson (1969) led to significantly higher grades for those who attended than for controls who were initially rated more able, and their attrition rate was considerably lower. A study by Gardiner, Boddy and Taylor (1969) shows that in teaching applied pharmacology, anaesthesiology and hospital procedure, practical experience in the wards may with advantage be substituted for lectures. Among 74 senior dental students, the group which spent two days in normal surgical wards – where teaching was minimal, but practical experience and contact with all grades of hospital staff were at a maximum – required less time and found it easier to assimilate information than did the group which attended 22 lectures during a period of ten weeks (Stuebner and Johnson, 1969). Sandwich courses have been designed with these advantages in mind but few have been evaluated. In Canada, at Waterloo (Holmes, 1970) students of engineering who spend alternate terms in college and in industry are said to have an awareness of, and confidence in, the opportunities within Canadian industry which has led to a reduction in the brain drain to the United States. However, satisfaction with sandwich courses in engineering seems to be limited to some schools and some courses. Theoretical courses are often overloaded and about half the students in one inquiry found industrial training unsatisfactory (Howard et al., 1968).

Detailed studies of the uses of students' time over a period of a day or, more probably, a week, give a useful indication of the pressure or slackness of work, attendance at voluntary courses or other activities, etc., and so provide a basis for changes in the curriculum or, possibly in teaching methods. In an early study of this kind Thoday (1957) asked each of over 500 students in Birmingham University to account in detail for his or her activities on the previous day. Information was also obtained about main activities during the previous weekend and a proportion of students were interviewed twice to give some idea of day-to-day variations. She found that mean time spent in work per day was six and a quarter hours; three and a half hours in time-table work and the remaining two and three-quarter hours in 'informal work'. Contrary to belief, female and science students worked no harder than male or arts students, but the latter did more informal and less set work. Second year students worked least hard except those studying medicine and modern languages who had important examinations then. In most subjects students did more work in the first than in the final year. In an investigation among sixth formers, students at a college of education and a technical university, Child (1970) found no difference in their study habits except that sixth formers worked more at week-ends.

Recent studies are far more detailed. Students are asked to account for time hourly during the night and quarter hourly during the day and to fill in their schedule using code numbers for different activities during one week. Mean times may be compared with estimates provided in advance by teachers. In one medical school (Anderson et al., 1968), clinical students proved to be working 40 to 50 hours per week but preferred to take more leisure throughout the week and to work during part of the weekend; the first years averaged seven hours per day, while second years averaged six hours. Teachers' estimates corresponded fairly well with average times given to different activities by students except that they supposed students talked shop more than they claimed to do and that they spent far less time in leisure activities than, in fact, they did. The authors concluded that the failure of students to work hard suggested that the course could be more challenging.

In an unpublished study in another clinical department a similar questionnaire was completed and a sample of students were also observed throughout a period of three weeks. Staff supposed that the first year students would spend some

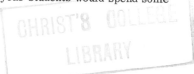

seven to eight hours per day in the wards or in study, but their mean time in the hospital proved to be 4·6 hours daily including lunch-hour, and with little evidence of additional work. In the observer's opinion the students felt insufficiently involved, at least during this period, to work hard in their clinical course.

RECALL AND RETENTION OF INFORMATION

Experiments Based on the Findings of Psychologists

Methods of improving immediate recall, or retention, of subject matter are based on what is known of remembering and forgetting in learning. It is known that to assist memory subject matter should be meaningful, inter-relationships between topics should be stressed, and frequent short periods should be spent in study in preference to a few long ones. Forgetting on the other hand, is induced by presenting the learner with many unrelated details, or by interference where a new topic is introduced at the end of a period of study or if two closely similar topics are learned together. To encourage accurate recall, correct responses should be rewarded or reinforced immediately (possibly only by knowing that the response is right) while wrong responses should be corrected at once. It is commonly said that errors should be avoided as far as possible. Above all, it is important that the student should make a response, though it may be a purely mental one; to be efficient, his learning must actively employ his ability to organize new information into his existing mental schemes. Where learning takes place by rote, with little understanding, subsequent forgetting is rapid. Obviously interest is also important; a student who is interested is more likely to play an active part in teaching himself.

Studies in which principles are stressed while details are reduced in number take account of these findings. Erskine and O'Morchoe compared recall following a course in anatomy in which principles were stressed and details omitted with one of the same length in which details were included (Erskine and O'Morchoe, 1961). But although results appear to be consistent with findings in the psychology of learning, the experiment was performed with groups which were not strictly comparable, since they were in different years and were, presumably, taught by different teachers.

Adams, Daniel, Herxheimer and Weatherall made a controlled study into the value of emphasis in the elimination of errors, collecting common errors, testing them on a group of 53 students, and dividing them for the purposes of the experiment into matched groups (Adams et al., 1960). For the next few months in the experimental group each misconception was deliberately discredited whenever it was relevant to mention it, while misconceptions in the control group received no special attention. At the end of the course, incidence of misconceptions of the experimental (emphasized) items had decreased by a highly significant amount as compared with incidence of misconceptions in control items. Thus there was no support for the common belief among teachers that emphasizing errors leads to their perpetuation.

An unexpected finding in this experiment was that the students who attended best had the highest incidence of misconceptions initially. The best attenders showed substantial improvement during the course both on treated and untreated items; moderate attenders improved only on treated items, and the poor attenders showed little improvement, what little there was being mainly in the treated items. Broadly, this provides evidence that the first group were probably the most intelligent who were sensitive even to slight emphases. The writers consider of special interest that this group of students 'entered the experiment with the highest incidence of misconceptions and finished with the lowest – that is, the best learners went through a phase of putting forward the selected misconceptions unusually readily'. They suggest that this points to a trial and error mechanism of learning, lending support to the saying 'If you don't make mistakes you won't make anything'.

Some light is cast on the seeming contradiction in this experiment (to the belief that it is unwise to emphasize errors), from the results of an experiment by Elley who contrasted the effect of errors in rote and logical tasks (1966). He used multiple choice questions allowing different rates of error in the course of learning each task. In rote learning, frequent errors resulted in inaccurate recall but, in logical tasks, the rate of error made no difference for, in these cases, students did not tend to repeat errors which they happened to have made while learning. Elley comments that, in preparing programmed texts for students on meaningful learning tasks, there is no need to be restricted by the assumption that errors must be kept to a minimum due to the interference they occasion in learning. However, in simpler tasks such as acquisition of vocabulary and elementary use of language, methods which lead to error-free learning are the most effective.

Avoidance of interference due to the order of presentation of learning tasks was studied by Leith and McHugh (1967). The questions they wished to answer were whether it was preferable to present a familiar task first, following it with an unfamiliar one as is usually advised by teachers, or whether the reverse would result in more effective learning and, in either case, where to introduce a theoretical passage explaining the subject. Students studying anthropology were given three passages: kinship systems of patrilineal and matrilineal tribes and a theoretical passage explaining the significance of kinship and different patterns of marriage, descent and residence. The design of the experiment allowed eight treatments with 80 students; the passages were studied during three 45-minute sessions in one day and a test containing items from all three passages was administered two days later. Analysis of the results showed that students did equally well in questions relating to the familiar, patrilineal system whatever the order of presentation, but they recalled the matrilineal system significantly better if it was presented before the more familiar system, and theory was helpful only if it came between these passages or at the end.

Feedback in Learning

The use of continuous feedback as to the success of learning is likewise an essential feature of programmed learning. But prompt and frequent feedback is recommended almost equally by other psychologists as an aid to recall and retention of information. Asking questions of students during the lecture period to which they must write the answers, and providing correct answers immediately proves to be an extremely effective method of teaching (Beard, 1967b). McCarthy (1968) gave feedback to his students by using a step-by-step lecture method in which each of ten or more questions projected on a screen was attempted by the students and discussed by the lecturer before proceeding. The students were supplied with a handout of questions for each lecture to provide a complete record and on which they could write notes. They were generally in favour of the method. It is interesting that the lecturer underestimated the time needed to discuss earlier questions and overestimated students' preknowledge. Thus it seems that feedback to the lecturer during discussion made him slow down to a pace appropriate to the students' ease of understanding.

An adaptable form of feedback to the teacher with minimal expense called the 'Cosford Cube' has been used by Taplin with RAF trainees (1969). Students were each provided with a two and a half inch cube with differently coloured faces which could be held so that a chosen colour visible only to the instructor indicated the answer to a multiple-choice question. Taplin recommends its use both after making critical points and at the end of a lecture; but he found that lectures took longer and required more preparation. Dunn obtained similar results with medical students using coloured cards (1969).

Elton (Elton et al., 1970) also reports the value to students of receiving lecture notes and self-testing devices. Students read and revised more and could follow lectures better. Provision of full lecture notes in a basic science course for first year undergraduates brought benefits to staff also, for they saw for the first time what their colleagues were teaching and were able to integrate courses. Although notes were provided in advance, lectures were well attended and students expected their lecturers to talk around the subject.

MacManaway (1970) discarded lectures, substituting lecture scripts and giving questions and assignments designed to test students' comprehension and to extend their thinking in sociology. Feedback was first obtained by substituting discussion in seven or eight groups of three or four students during the first half-hour of lecture time, and then by general discussion and elucidation when leaders reported their groups' findings. 90 per cent of the students found the method stimulating and enjoyable, 93 per cent commented on the value of discussions, 64 per cent said they had learned to use sociological ideas and terminology and only 13 per cent preferred some kind of lecture; but 58 per cent still said they felt uncertain what information was important.

Television seems an unlikely medium for the use of audience participation and feedback to the student, but Gane (1969), having presented his objectives on the screen, gave information and then asked a question or posed a problem. A carefully judged length of time was allowed for each viewer to work out his response before the answer was given on the screen and discussed. If the problems are carefully chosen — as in a programmed sequence — the student's answer book should provide a valuable record of key issues. This technique may also be used in a lecture, but in both cases subsequent discussion to remove misconceptions is advisable.

Applying information is also an aid to retention. McLeish found that students recalled only 42 per cent of the content of a lecture immediately afterwards but, if they received a copy of the lecture and applied its contents soon after hearing the lecture, they retained three quarters of what they had learned after one month (McLeish, 1968).

Activity in Learning

The importance of activity on the part of the learner is a principle of learning
as it is described by the field psychologists; they describe learning in terms of
the individual sizing up, or interpreting, his world in a way that is meaningful to
him, integrating experiences into existing organizations of knowledge and using
the environment in ways advantageous to him. It follows that what the individual
perceives is selective. In teaching, therefore, field psychologists are concerned
with motivation, stress the importance of arranging that learning experiences
are organized into meaningful wholes, and favour the use of problem situations
which enable the learner to gain 'insight' as he suddenly realizes how to use
information or how to interpret it meaningfully. In addition, the learner may
develop and follow his own goals. Their more self-directed, problem-centred
approach may be thought of as most suited to practical laboratory work or in
teaching students to work independently by providing problems or topics for
them to study alone; but it also aids recall and retention of information, probably
because in the course of the student's activities he integrates information
meaningfully into what he already knows so making it easier to retrieve when it
is needed since many bonds have been formed with other knowledge. Holland
et al. (1968) used practical experience to make clinical students aware of social
and emotional aspects of medical care by assigning each student in the experimental group a patient from the ante-natal clinic to visit and attend during the
following seven months. These students also prepared reports on such topics
as family size by social class within the area, etc., while the control group
followed a conventional course. In a multiple choice test given unexpectedly,
both groups did about equally well in clinical obstetrics but the experimental
group was significantly superior in knowledge of social medicine.

It is relevant here that one of the main criticisms of the lecture by medical
students is that it is a passive method of learning (British Medical Students
Association, 1965); many of them wish a large proportion of lectures to be
replaced by teaching methods allowing more student participation and, in the
lectures that remain, they advocate a more extensive use of audio-visual techniques so providing for simultaneous auditory and visual learning.

In contrast, there is some evidence from recent work of the value of relaxation
in learning. Repin and Orlov (1967), reporting experiments in an Australian
journal, claimed that when two-three hours were allowed for conventional learning
some 70-80 per cent of 50 new English words were recalled on the average
immediately afterwards, with a range of 40-100 per cent; but, in a state of
relaxation, 20 minutes sufficed for students to attain scores of 80-88 per cent
and, after a further five minutes of visual rehearsal this rose to 92-98 per cent.
Three months later 90-94 per cent of words learned in relaxation but only
50-60 per cent of words learned conventionally, could be recalled by the
students. Special suggestion to memorize improved performance further. The
editors comment however, that it is difficult to assess the experiment as full
information is lacking and there were no statistical tests.

The importance of activity on the part of the student is also one of the tenets
of those who design programmes for machines and programmed books.
Influenced by the behaviourist school of psychology they concentrate their

attention on changes in overt performance and describe learning as built up by reinforcement of responses to stimuli from the environment, though these may, of course, be consequent upon the learner's activity. The learner should therefore be encouraged to follow a logically organized sequence of stimuli, including questions, with feedback as to his success serving to reinforce correct responses.

Programmed Learning

A number of studies show that programmed learning is at least as effective as traditional teaching. When Orr (1968) tested sailors for the retention of information about atomic structure one day, one week and two weeks after tuition, there was no significant difference between those taught by programmed learning and those taught by conventional lectures. Farrell (1965) found a notable increase in retention of information, giving a 49 per cent lower failure rate for the programmed learning group, in an examination in the Royal Canadian Air Force but in these cases the topics were fairly elementary. Yet at university level, it appears to be almost as successful. Guild (1966) has reported the successful use of a programme for individual teaching in dentistry. Jamieson, James and Leytham (1969) compared programmed learning, lectures well augmented with visual aids, and 'straight lectures' in educational psychology given to 184 postgraduate students. Post-tests showed significant differences in learning in the order stated and the superiority of programmed learning was still apparent on a test five months later when there was no apparent difference in the effect of the two styles of lecture. At no stage was there a significant correlation with the student's intelligence, sex, estimated teaching ability, arts or science background. Buckley-Sharp et al. (1969) found programmed learning groups significantly superior to a group given introductory notes in a test of biochemistry administered three weeks later.

Manning, Abrahamson and Dennis (1968) who compared a programmed text, a well-illustrated textbook, a formal lecture punctuated by demonstrations and a lecture supplemented by problem-solving exercises under supervision, showed there were no significant differences in learning measured by a multiple-choice test, but the two lecture methods took significantly longer.

Programmed Courses

Stavert (1966, 1969) found that a course based exclusively on programmes resulted in 10 per cent lower test scores and unpopularity of the method compared with conventional teaching; but popularity, test scores and motivation improved when a variety of techniques including tutorials and laboratory-work were used. He concludes that programmed learning must be part of a system of instruction which allows for human interaction. Croxton and Martin (1965 and 1967) replaced courses in Strength of Materials and Theory of Structures by two theories of short programmes together with problems and tests to follow each programme. The programmes were progressively modified according to difficulties recorded by students on a standard form. Their students preferred being taught both subjects this way, finding them fairly easy whereas formerly they were among the most difficult; but they wished contact with the tutors to be maintained, and desired a measure of competition with other students. Problems and difficulties were therefore considered in tutorials six days after receiving the programmes, and lectures were replaced by tests on which the student had to score 90 per cent before receiving the next programme. The time spent on these courses, as compared with others, suggests that the tests, the pressure to be ready for tutorials, and the inclusion of test-results in their final assessment increased motivation. Performance in sessional examinations was better than it had been with conventional teaching. Castle and Davidson (1969) concluded that programmed learning was 'effective to bring groups of people varying widely in social, ethnic and academic backgrounds in a new medical faculty, to the same high level of attainment' at the beginning of a course.

Co-operation in working problems

There appears to be conflicting evidence on whether programmes are best studied individually, in pairs or in larger groups. James Hartley (1968) has argued that although self-pacing is an important principle in programmed learning, learning alone is sometimes not as effective as working in pairs. Dick (1963) using a programme on algebra 3,500 frames long with 34 university students, found that individuals worked quicker and, although there was no difference when tested at first, students who worked in pairs scored better on a test one year later. Since, apart from two experiments (Amaria et al., 1969; Amaria and Leith, 1969), work with school children does not show the same results, it is tempting to speculate whether age, intellectual or co-operative abilities are important variables. James (1970) used a branching programme on management with individuals and with unpaced groups of three or four apprentices or managers and, although the short term results favoured individual learning, the difference was much less after four weeks. There is some evidence that discussion methods favour long term retention compared with conventional methods of teaching and this may explain the findings of both Dick and James in the context of programmed learning. There appears to be little difference between working individually and in a group larger than three, perhaps because the usual method of displaying the frames for a group by projection to a screen does not easily permit discussion of each response by the students. Thus it may be the opportunity for discussion that is important, rather than the size of the co-operative group.

Although one of the basic principles of programmed learning is that students should work at their own pace, a number of experiments in which programmes have been presented to a whole group requiring students to keep pace with its others members, do not show any significant deterioration in learning. When Moore (1967) used a programme on 53 students of physiological psychology there was no difference in test results between those who learned in a group and those that worked individually with booklets. Moore argues that although the average time taken by individuals was 77 minutes and by the group 87 minutes, group presentation has advantages if programmed learning is used in class where all must wait for the slowest. James Hartley (1968) reviews a number of studies, comparing individual use of a booklet with film strip or TV projection of an algebra programme to a group; most showed no significant difference between the two methods. But Gallegos (1968) found that both high and low ability students learned better if they did programmes at their own speed, or were paced at a speed slower than the class average, than if they were made to go faster than usual. Stones (1966), who experimented with programmed learning to see whether supervision, working in a group, or working to a set time influenced results or attitudes, found no differences between five groups except that students working independently took more time, probably because they lacked the stimulus of competition.

Branching programmes

Glynn (1965), and Hoare and Inglis (1965) used teaching programmes in chemistry with HNC students and first year MB students respectively. The HNC students liked the method and did well in compulsory questions in their examinations, weaker students showing the greatest gains. The majority of the first year MB students reported that they found the programmes useful, or very useful, for increasing comprehension, revision and answering problems and the class as a whole did exceptionally well in the organic chemistry examination. Glynn made use of both linear and branching methods. (A linear programme is a single ordered succession of frames − usually statements with a word missing − and proceeds by very easy stages. The answer to each frame is provided either at the beginning of the next one or overleaf. Since there is no provision for the correction of errors the programme must necessarily consist of short steps which are easy to answer correctly. A branching programme offers a choice of answers and students proceed to different frames according to the answer they select. They are told whether they were right or wrong and why; thus they proceed by different paths and at different speeds. In the branching programme frames may be fairly long.) In a further study with first year MB and dental students, Hoare and Revans (1969) used objective tests based on Bloom's (1956) first three levels of objectives. Compared with a pre-test they found that a student's knowledge of facts, theories and formulae increased 70 per cent, their ability to use them increased 50 per cent and their ability to apply them in new or unfamiliar situations increased by 43 per cent. Performance of individual students at the different levels indicated that ability to recall knowledge and power to apply it were relatively distinct abilities. Using 268 university students Pikas (1969) compared programmed learning with traditional teaching in which the students had to answer questions, and traditional teaching where the students were passive listeners, by immediately testing some students on their factual knowledge and its application, and testing the others on its application the next day. He found that programmed learning was superior for immediate tests of factual knowledge, traditional teaching was superior where the students had to answer questions of application, but there was little difference where the traditional teaching required the student to be a passive listener. Both kinds of traditional teaching were superior on tests of application given the next day when compared with programmed learning. Unlike Hoare and Revans', the programme used by Pikas did not require students to apply the knowledge they had learned. Pikas argues that the greater the dissimilarity between the learning and task situations, the greater the superiority of traditional teaching. We may conclude that if one wishes students to apply the information they learn, they must be taught to do so.

The advantage of branching programmes is that they provide feed-back specific to the needs of the students; but Stones (1967) has argued that since 'all the branches and remedial sequences are related to a hypothesized best linear path', and feedback in linear programmes can be amplified beyond mere confirmation, there is no important difference between the two forms of programme. Senter et al. (1966) found that only six per cent of the possible 'wrong' branches were used with Crowder's original programme, 'Arithmetic of Computers'. Kaufman (1963) found no significant difference in the amount of remedial material between the two different kinds of programme. When Biran (1966) and Biran and Pickering (1968) 'unscrambled' a branching programme it took less time to do with no decrease in learning. The answers to questionnaires showed that sixth form and adult students prefer a straightforward presentation. Biran suggests that searching through a scrambled book may hinder learning, whilst this is avoided if a machine is used; but three out of four studies reviewed by Tobin showed no significant advantage in machine presentation of branching programmes. Tobin concludes that the major variable affecting the success of the programme is the quality of the original task analysis and, while the machine can act as an attention-focusing device for younger and less able students, machines are no better than a programmed text for the average student. It is possible that branching programmes have a particular role where the objective is to improve the student's powers of judgement (Peel, 1967). Tobin's conclusion is confirmed by Owen et al. (1965), who, in a carefully designed experiment, compared a branching programme in teaching electro-cardiography with a course of lectures specially prepared to correspond with the programmed material. They found no interaction between method and academic ability nor between method and sex. Less able students profited most from using teaching machines, but the women in this group did better when taught by lectures. Overall, the two groups spent about equal times in study, but the majority of students preferred machines to lectures.

Programmes with other methods

A number of studies have compared different methods of programme presentation. Using Owen's programme Stretton, Hall and Owen (1967) compared the use of teaching machines and programmed textbooks, and found that the machines took insignificantly longer and there was no difference in their effectiveness. Conner (1968) also found no difference with engineers, but groups using machines and programmed texts both did better than controls in the annual examination. Tobin summarized 19 studies comparing machine and a textbook presentation of linear programmes and found one to the advantage of each, and 17 where there was no significant difference. Poppleton and Austwick (1964) compared a programme in elementary statistics with reading and note-taking but found that the learning of pairs of matched students was about equally effective by either method. After comparing the use of an individual programmed booklet with a programme presented frame by frame on to a screen for a longer time than it takes 60 per cent of the class to respond, Moore (1967) concludes that the group method can save time in conventional teaching situations, requires only one programme, is cheaper than individual machines and can be used as part of a conventional lesson. However, this requires the presence of a teacher, whereas individual work with programmes does not.

James (1970) compared a programmed video-tape plus a handout with the use of an instruction booklet; students preferred the video-tape, but their learning was marginally better with the booklet. Comparing a tape-recorded presentation of a programme on the operation of machine tools with a similar written version, Amswych (1967) found the oral presentation both quicker and more effective. Evidence that learning from programmes in paragraphs can be more effective than learning from brief frames was obtained by Wright (1967). She designed an experiment in which undergraduates worked through a section of a programmed text of psychology prepared in one of four ways: in short frames with blanks, paragraphs followed by questions, or frames or paragraphs with answers filled in. Completed frames proved significantly more effective than those with blanks, and paragraphs were significantly more effective than frames, paragraphs with questions being by far the most effective. She suggested that the structure of this material was more clear in paragraphs. Williams (1963) confirmed the importance of making a written response, but Krumboltz (1964) found no significant difference between students using a conventional programme with written responses and those reading prose, in either an immediate or a delayed test, while in an earlier experiment (Krumboltz and Weisman, 1962) he found superior recall in the response group after two weeks.

The form of response

A different kind of inquiry using programmed learning was made by Leith and Buckle (1966) who studied the effect of overt or covert responses to frames in relation to difficulty of material. Following the use of a programme in electronics with three groups of students formed on the basis of prior knowledge (A-level physics at least, O-level at least, or little knowledge of physics), they concluded that the more difficult the task was to the learner, the greater was the need for overt responses. But, in line with the well known findings that rote learning is more efficient when it takes place vocally rather than mentally, they found that overt responses were in general more effective than covert ones. This is an interesting finding in view of the experimental results with younger children.

Basing their work on Piaget's observations (1926), Slavina and Galparin (1957) have used in teaching a gradual internalization of information or concepts from use of concrete materials with instructions spoken out loud, whispered, then thought, and, possibly, in a final stage forgotten, as a successful operation is carried out. When the level of difficulty is sufficiently great it seems that adult students too may learn more effectively if they respond overtly at first, gradually internalizing their responses.

The traditional reason given for this is that overt responses are more strongly reinforcing than covert ones but Sime and Boyce (1969) in an important, well designed experiment concluded that questions raised the level of students' attention, for non-reinforced concepts were also learned better when questions were asked.

The Lecture

a Function

Inquiries in connection with the Hale Report (University Grants Committee, 1964) show that the views of university teachers in Britain on lecturing are more favourable than those in the medical students' report (British Medical Students' Association, 1965). Most of them believe that students are too immature to study independently and that lectures are the most economical way of communicating information to them. Scientists, in particular, regard the lecture as an excellent way to introduce and to open up difficult topics which students cannot undertake on their own, while it is generally felt that the lecture is the only solution to a paucity of books or rapid developments in subject matter which outdate existing books. Nearly all teachers claim to cover the syllabus in broad scope and principle, using only sufficient illustration for the principle to be understood. They point out also that they can respond to the students in a way that teaching aids cannot, that they are able to show their students how to organize a topic or how to build up a complex argument or diagram, and that they can share their enthusiasm for the subject, include discussion of recent developments or indicate topics for further inquiry.

The comments of students consulted in Marris' inquiry (1965) that they desired lectures to be clear, orderly synopses, logically planned, emphasizing basic principles and with not too many digressions, and that time should not be wasted in imparting the contents of the text-book, suggest that lecturers may be less successful than they believe in using lectures to impart knowledge in these ways. The high percentages (over 40 per cent) commenting adversely on delivery and clarity of exposition tend to confirm this. On the other hand, there is evidence that some students share the lecturers' more favourable view of the lecture. In the study by Joyce and Weatherall (1959) comparing four methods of teaching, the students considered lectures outstandingly the most useful, demonstrations following some way behind, with seminars a close third and practicals a close fourth. But students of the Royal Dental Hospital School of Dental Surgery in their opinion poll on lectures showed less agreement (Students' Society Committee, 1966). There was no consistent view as to the value of lectures nor as to how courses might be improved. The only conclusion which could be drawn with confidence from this part of the inquiry was that more lectures would be unpopular. There was no doubt, however, that students of the School expected lectures to fulfil three functions: to introduce the subject and set it in its context, to bring the text-book up to date and to provide discussion of problems and their possible solutions.

In the NUS report of 1969 (Saunders et al.), students thought the major functions of lectures were to impart information (76 per cent), to provide a framework for the course (75 per cent), to indicate methods of approaching the subject (64 per cent), to indicate sources of reference (47 per cent) and to stimulate independent work (41 per cent). They criticized the hindrance to understanding necessitated by note-taking, frequent repetition of standard text-books and poor preparation and presentation. Distribution of duplicated notes by the lecturer was strongly advocated to overcome the first of these.

Maclaine (1965), in surveying teaching methods in Australian universities, grouped the advantages and disadvantages under these headings: motivational, organizational and informational-elucidatory. In addition to listing most of the points made in the Hale Report he included under the first heading exploration of desirable by-ways, under the second, guidance in reading and evaluation of text-books and, under the third, 'to explore and clarify ideas and techniques'. But an adverse effect of the comprehensive course of lectures in an Australian university school is mentioned by Schonell, Roe and Middleton (1962) who comment that although teachers may sincerely believe that their lectures serve as a guide to reading they are, in fact, used by some students as a wholly self-sufficient course of study; in their survey, 15 per cent of Queensland students relied almost entirely on lecture notes and the majority of students studied primarily from them.

Bligh (a) has used objective tests at eight cognitive levels to evaluate lectures in psychology. Tests of terminology, facts, general principles and simple comprehension showed comparable gains; skill in applying knowledge showed varied increases while improvements in analysis, synthesis and evaluation of information were negligible. Furthermore, although it might be expected that students with previous knowledge and comprehension of the subject, as measured by a pre-test, could use the occasion to think more deeply about it, they did no better in the post-test on questions requiring higher levels of thinking. These findings suggest that lectures can best be used to convey information and that they are not occasions during which much thought occurs, at least as they are currently organized.

Whether lectures should be compulsory or not is a matter to be decided consistently with the aims of the school or department. In some schools encouragement of independence in students is valued so highly that some inefficiency is countenanced as a result of absence; but that absentees from lectures do less well in tests and exams, than those who attend has been shown in several studies (Adams et al., 1960; Holloway, 1966). Where it is impossible to make good the loss of information in lectures, compulsory attendance would generally be recommended.

b Place and Length

The place of the lecture differs in the various faculties. At the time of the Hale Report, in 1964, arts faculties used mainly lectures and discussion groups, with reading, whereas in the science faculties there were more lectures with practical or laboratory periods but comparatively little discussion. In arts the average weekly hours spent in lectures were 6.8 from a total of 10.1 hours of instruction, in pure science 8.3 of 17.3 hours and, in applied sciences, both lecture time and total time spent in instruction were still higher viz. 10.7 and 19.6 hours (University Grants Committee, 1964). During the last few years, however, there has been a considerable increase in the use of small discussion groups in departments of science and mathematics (Beard, 1967 a).

In law there is a similar trend. A survey of legal education in 1966 shows that the majority of lecturers agree that some lectures are essential but they would welcome the extension of the tutorial system to at least two tutorials per week (Wilson, 1966). They also consider that students should have more opportunity to sample law in action in courts and solicitors' offices, subsequently discussing their visits.

There is little experimental work on the lecture from British sources. Holloway (1966) compared recall of information in dentistry among groups of first and third-year students attending lectures at 9 a.m. or 4.30 p.m. Analysis of scores in two ways, comparing students with themselves on different occasions, or students with each other in the same test items, showed significant superiority for classes held in the morning.

McLeish (1966) was interested in the problem whether students listening to only the first twenty minutes of a lecture would remember more of it than those who were present for 40 minutes or one hour due to interferences set up by later material. He used three experimental groups who attended different lengths of lecture and a control group who did not attend. Overall the experimental group recalled 42 per cent of what they had heard as measured by an objective test immediately afterwards, but the hypothesis that there would be loss of recall due to retroactive interference was not borne out. This may perhaps be explained by a difference in content of the three parts of the lecture but further experiment is needed to determine in what ways later material may vary before it causes retroactive interference. In theory there should be minimal retro-active interference with the final part of a lecture and this receives some support from an experiment by Johnston and Calhoun (1969). Using a short tape-recorded talk and multiple-choice questions with 269 students, they found that material at the beginning and end of a talk was better remembered than the central sections no matter in what order the information was presented. In the experiment by Trenaman, quoted by McLeish, listeners to a 45-minutes talk on Astronomy assimilated appreciably less after the first fifteen minutes and, after thirty minutes, ceased to take in anything additional or forgot what they had memorized earlier. However, it is impossible to generalize from the results of a single experiment of this kind even if we know the subject matter, the manner of presentation, and the difficulty of the subject to the participants. Lloyd (1968) compared the number of facts noted by students during each period of ten minutes during a lecture. He concluded that after an initial increase, there was a steady decline until the last ten minutes, and that those planning lectures should bear this in mind.

Observation suggests that a lecture given at a suitable speed in mathematics or certain science topics, in which a logical presentation is written on the blackboard, provides constant opportunity to the student to obtain feedback on his understanding of the topic; for, unless the speed is too great, he can work out the next line just in advance of the lecturer, obtaining confirmation, or correction, as soon as that line is written. Inability to obtain reinforce-ment in this way is probably the chief cause of frustration when the lecturer proceeds too fast or presents material in a disorderly fashion.

c Delivery

There does not appear to be any British experimental work on techniques of delivering lectures; but views expressed in inquiries have some interest as there is often a high level of agreement. Students of the Royal Dental Hospital School of Dental Surgery comment (Students' Society Committee, 1966): "a lecture has to be delivered very very slowly indeed before the speed is found to be too slow but only a moderate increase in pace will produce com-plaints of 'too fast'." However, they remark on inconsistencies in views as to suitability of speed in delivering orthodentics lectures: 44 per cent of the fourth year, seven per cent of the fifth year and 80 per cent of the sixth year find the speed unsuitable; possibly this reflects the anxiety of students at the approach of an examination, but it may also be affected by the difficulty of the subject at each level and perhaps suggests that speed should vary inversely with difficulty of material. This is consistent with an experiment by Bligh (d) who gave identical lectures to three groups at different speeds. Results of multiple-choice tests at eight cognitive levels showed significant interaction between speed and subject matter on questions requiring more thought, but differences at lower cognitive levels and for speed alone were not significant. Interestingly, he found (Bligh, c) that tape recorded lectures could be taken twice as fast as the same lectures delivered by a teacher in person. Speed may also be a factor which influences students to say (NUS, 1969; Marris, 1965) that the major criticism of the lecture method is that 'the opportunity to grasp basic ideas is hindered by the necessity to take notes'. If so, the finding by Gust and Schumacher (1969) that writing speeds of female students are significantly faster than those of their male counterparts has relevance to lectures as well as examinations.

It is generally agreed that a lecture is more effective if it is spoken freely rather than read and that repetition is helpful in aiding subsequent recall. It is also advantageous to supplement the spoken word by visual aids where these are relevant. But lecturing styles tend to be stereotyped despite the case for variety and enterprise. (Bligh, 1970). To help and interest first year students taking a compulsory 'structure and properties of matter' course, Betts and Walton (1970) gave lectures together as a dialogue to nearly 400 students at a time, using television monitors for demonstrations and illustrations in two lecture theatres. Betts provided the logical outline with Walton interposing awkward questions and conducting demonstrations or experiments. They report that although the brighter students might have preferred a more rapid presentation, on the whole students were favourable. The dialogue lecture merits wider use since differences of opinion can be expressed and contrasting voices maintain student attention. At the same time one may question the widespread practice of obliging such large audiences to listen to the same content despite a very wide range in ability and prior knowledge.

d Evaluation

Evaluation of teaching methods in general is dealt with in a later section but some comments specific to the lecture are appropriate here. It is not easy to evaluate a lecture, taking into account all its objectives, and it would probably be undesirable to attempt to evaluate each lecture of a series. Nevertheless some evaluation appears to be worthwhile. Few of the heads of departments consulted as to the success of lectures in an Australian inquiry were satisfied that objectives were achieved (Australian Vice-Chancellors Committee, 1963); they commented that lectures tended to succeed with certain students but not with others or that lectures were more successful in certain subjects than in others. Whereas these differences seem inevitable, students complain of basic faults such as poor preparation, that lectures are neither clear nor systematic, so ill-delivered as to be barely audible, or that they are addressed to the professor's notes or to the blackboard. Others report lectures delivered so rapidly that they cannot be followed coherently, consisting of a mass of detail, or presenting a difficult argument in a fashion which only the most able students can follow.

Despite these varied criticisms it is probably true that almost all lecturers sincerely desire that their lectures should be well delivered and readily comprehensible. Failure in these respects is often unconscious and students of undergraduate age often fail to provide the hints, or outspoken criticisms, which would result in improved practice on the part of the lecturer. In the belief that most lecturers would welcome any means of finding out to what extent they were successful, a group of scientists working in a research group with the University Teaching Methods Research Unit of the University of London Institute of Education prepared a questionnaire for use by students. They invited them to agree with various statements, on a five-point scale, relating to the lecturer's audibility, speed and quality of delivery, appearance, manner and rapport with the class and to aspects of presentation of subject matter or use of audio-visual aids as well as to comment on surroundings and other factors influencing the success of the lecture. It is of interest that even among these enthusiasts it was not until nearly a year later that any of the group agreed to use the questionnaire; for, as one lecturer said: 'It will only give the students an opportunity to make satirical comments.' Yet when it was tried at the beginning of courses enthusiastic reports were sent in. A veterinary scientist reported that his students 'seemed grateful that something was being done' and that they combined to give a joint criticism and made useful suggestions. An electrical engineer (McVey, 1967) tried two forms of questionnaire with small groups; he discovered that there was more extraneous noise than he had supposed and that on changing from lectures with notes to lectures without notes he had not slowed his pace sufficiently; he received confirmation of information obtained in earlier surveys that his students liked duplicated notes and coloured diagrams since they found the latter clearer than the blackboard and the former enabled them to concentrate better on the lecture. A biologist received approximately 80 per cent response from a large class and felt that it had been particularly valuable to receive criticisms and comments at the beginning of a course since it enabled her to adapt her teaching to their needs in the remaining lectures. Although this technique does not inform the teacher how much the students are learning, it does establish better rapport and almost certainly results in more efficient teaching.

This is one satisfactory method to use but it is not the only one. Among methods reported within the University of London are the following: taping a lecture and listening to it subsequently in private, taping a lecture and observing in the next class while they listen to the recording, inviting students to provide immediate feed-back on the lecturer's success by complaints as to excessive speed, lack of explanation of difficult points etc. and, in a few cases, lecturers invite colleagues to attend their lectures and to criticize them. A number of other methods used in American Schools are outlined in an article by Simpson (1965).

Smithers (1970 a) asked 431 university students at the end of their second year to rate 50 possible characteristics of the ideal lecturer. Students in all fields of study were agreed that the ideal lecturer is an authority in his subject and can expound it clearly, that he thoroughly prepares his lectures, gives them an obvious framework and is ready to respond to questions. In other respects there were differences in emphasis according to field of study: students of applied science and engineering appeared to look towards lectures for information, social scientists, for stimulation. These differences in emphasis suggest that teaching and lecturing abilities may be more specific than is commonly supposed.

Smithers (1970 c) also found that extraverts attached more importance to the lecture as a performance; for them the ideal lecturer is entertaining, confident and at ease. Those more 'unstable' as measured by the Eysenck Personality Inventory want the lecturer to be as definite and certain as possible and to give full notes, whilst dogmatic students are most concerned that the lecturer should keep to the point, set clear goals and convey the information lucidly.

In an earlier inquiry by Cooper and Foy (1967), students and staff in a university department of pharmacy were asked to put statements describing lecturers' characteristics in order of importance. The first 10 for the students, in order, were as follows: 1. presents his material clearly and logically; 2. enables the student to understand the basic principle of the subject; 3. can be clearly heard; 4. makes his material intelligibly meaningful; 5. adequately covers the ground in the lecture course; 6. maintains continuity in the course; 7. is constructive and helpful in his criticism; 8. shows an expert knowledge of his subject; 9. adopts an appropriate pace in his lectures; 10. includes in his lectures materials which are not readily accessible in text books. Staff and student ratings correlated quite highly (.77); but, whereas students valued adequate coverage of the course, attempts to link theory with laboratory and practical work, even spacing of requirements for written work, and humour, staff were much more concerned with avoidance of excess factual detail. Two and a half years later Foy (1969) repeated the inquiry with a different set of students and found a correlation with the judgements of their predecessors of 0.93 which certainly confirms the reliability, though not necessarily the validity, of students' judgements.

Audio-visual Aids

In view of the widespread use of audio-visual aids in university teaching the number of investigations to determine their value in British university schools is rather few. A recent monography by Flood Page (1971) reviews the available literature in greater detail than is possible here and the inquiring reader is advised to refer to it. It is true that some advances due to new techniques are so great that experiments are unnecessary to demonstrate them – the transmission of a lecture to millions instead of hundreds, for example, but if the value of the aid is in doubt experiments are desirable. Unfortunately, where experiments have been made their results are too little publicized so that the complaint that it takes thirty years for the findings of educational experiments to be put into practice is sometimes fully justified. In 1937, Seymour (1937) showed that a light-coloured board with dark lettering was more efficient than the familiar black-board and chalk; both children and adults could read dark blue letters from a pale yellow board some 15 per cent faster than chalk letters from a blackboard, while the children could copy from it in 10 per cent less time. Nevertheless, it was not until 1966 that manufacturers displayed light boards with dark 'pencils'. Even then they cannot have experimented with them in a sample of schools, for the 'pencils' contained coloured fluids and would have proved irresistible to young artists and aspiring mechanics alike. Nevertheless, these findings should be known in university departments where boards are in constant use, e.g. in the mathematics departments; the use of the new boards would not only save students' time in note-taking but could avoid the deposit of chalk dust commonly found on lecture-room floors. More recently Foster (1968) used slides showing lower case letters and found that the maximum distance for 100 per cent correct identification was significantly superior with black letters on a white background than with white on black.

Probably the effect of dark lines on a light background is one reason for the popularity of the overhead projector; this combines the advantages of the blackboard, that the teacher can construct diagrams or notes as the lesson proceeds, with the further advantage of facing the class so that contact is not lost and adds the possibility of building up complex diagrams by use of successive, previously prepared, overlays. Apart from an experiment by Perlsberg and Resh (1967), quoted by Flood Page, (1971), in which the use of the OP was an advantage in geometry but not in hydrology, there has been little work comparing either its various uses, or its general effectiveness with that of other methods of presentation. Likewise, no experiments have been traced comparing these methods of presentation with each other or the overhead projector with the blackboard.

Audio tapes are comparatively cheap and, like television, have some self-evident advantages. In medicine (Graves and Graves, 1963) they enable students to listen to interviews between consultants and their patients which otherwise could be attended by, at most, one student; in conjunction with slides they are used to display the symptoms of diseases for the use of students overseas who lack teachers, or they may be borrowed by General Practitioners at home for revision, to acquaint themselves with new developments, or to learn to recognize symptoms of rare diseases (Graves and Graves, 1965 and 1967). In all of these cases the increase in efficiency is obvious; but, in university teaching, where a tape may be used to replace a lecture, experiments are necessary to determine which method is more successful.

Holloway (1964) compared a formal lecture demonstration of a practical procedure in conservative dentistry with instruction by a tape recording augmented by colour transparencies, using matched groups from a class of 22 students. No significant differences were found in capacity of the groups to carry out practical work or in retention of information after one month (in so small a sample differences would need to be very great to reach significance even at the five per cent level); but the tape-recorder group scored significantly higher in immediate recall of information. Possibly this superiority was due to the conciseness of the tape recording which enabled students to play it twice during the time taken for demonstrations.

Reduction in time for equivalent learning appears to be an advantage of tape-recorded instruction. In Bligh's experiment (Bligh c), students obtained comparable scores on post-tests although live lectures took about twice as long as identical tape-recorded talks. Students hearing recordings of lectures obtained better scores on multiple choice questions requiring some thought than those who heard the lecture live, or who had the same time to read the same words in a lecture script. A later experiment using audio-tape showed that a slower speed of delivery led to better scores on questions at higher cognitive levels.

Fletcher and Watson (1968) provided a tape-recorded commentary to lead four students simultaneously through an orderly microscopical examination of histopathological specimens. Their system includes the use of more than one voice to avoid monotony, sets of slides for each student and an optional replay device for the classroom with three channels carrying the same commentary, but progressively delayed. This enables students to spend longer viewing one slide and to resume on a later tape. They say the advantages of their system include greater accuracy and clarity of description, standardization and improvement of the histological examination, ease of revision and editing, active student participation and reduction of irregular, inconvenient teaching of small groups.

The use of tapes or books of information and questions, together with slides, have proved very effective in the teaching of veterinary science (Appleby and Poland, 1968).

A chance observation of preference for a tape-recording is mentioned in the Brynmor Jones Report (University Grants Committee...., 1965): a professor of mathematics prepared a lecture on probability theory in such a way that the mathematics was spoken in detail as it was written on the board in order to tape it for another class; when it was repeated with the other group the lecture proved 'surprisingly successful', the students finding the absence of the lecturer advantageous to some extent.

Tape has the further advantage that it is suited to individual use. A student who finds a topic difficult can repeat it until he knows it, so avoiding constant request to his teacher for help or interruptions to a class of students who are already competent. Tapes, with slides, are being prepared for these reasons in several of London's Dental Schools.

At Newcastle a windowless and otherwise non-functional room has been used to supplement conventional teaching methods by the provision of a synchronized stereo tape-recorder and slide projector which may be used individually or in groups. The synchrony is obtained by an impulse on the second channel of the tape-recorder activating the automatic projector. Carré (1969) provided audio-tapes in booths to supplement and dovetail with practicals and CCTV lectures, to promote deeper understanding by more able students, and to remedy deficiencies of weaker students or those with less background knowledge. He reports that students were enthusiastic, accepted responsibility for their own learning, and could progress at their own rate. A similar provision for up to 500 students of Economic Geography made by Woods and Northcott (1970) included lectures with a linear programme design, visual materials, multiple-choice questions and problems. Nearly all students preferred carrel learning to lectures. They liked to be able to go back over a point, felt more involved and, with a more flexible timetable, better communication between staff led to an improvement in the overall course structure. Compared with controls, fewer students using carrels failed, although slightly fewer obtained honours. New devices which make individual operation simpler are being prepared, for example, Harden et al. (1968) describe a device to record lectures synchronized with slides in an inexpensive and easily modified form. In a later experiment they compared a programmed tape-slide presentation with conventional teaching by lectures. Students taught in this way significantly improved their position in class and reacted favourably. Students found they were able to concentrate, the work was 'made easy' and the opportunity to work at their own speed was a particular advantage for those from overseas. However, they commented that the method was 'antisocial', too intensive and lacked humour!

Perhaps the most extensive development of tape in teaching is for use in language laboratories and other language teaching. Many teachers are now engaged in experiments applying the lessons and techniques of modern linguistics to the teaching of languages and to discover the best ways of using technological aids but, as yet, little of this work is even nearing completion.

Coggle (1968) and McNab, have investigated how behaviourist theories of stimulus-response bonds, the concept of reinforcement and maximum motivation, together with applied linguistics and audio-visual equipment, can help to solve the problem of teaching non-language specialists to understand and speak sufficient of a language to satisfy their particular needs in the shortest possible time. McNab made a pilot experiment in the teaching of German in 20 colleges throughout the country during 1964-5 and from this developed a course which was published in 1968 as the Ealing Course in German. Like programmed learning in other fields, objectives are elaborated in a form suitable for evaluation and the course consists of carefully graded exercises requiring constant responses from the student:

> 'The course is built up of the basic structures and linguistic items of modern standard spoken German. They are presented in situational context in a dialogue whose aim is to provide as naturally as possible a number of speech patterns appropriate to the situation to which the student can refer. These structures are next expanded in exercises based on a visual aid, then manipulated until overlearned in structure drills, and finally recombined and applied by the student in guided conversation. To give the student the intensive listening for comprehension practice required, every unit after Unit 3 has a listening passage associated in theme, structure patterns and vocabulary with the other material in the unit .....'

Information has been received by letter, and via a conference report, of other experiments in progress; those we mention may be taken as fairly representative of work throughout the country but it is by no means an exhaustive list. At

Birkbeck College, University of London, Dr. M. Blanc reports that the Language Research Centre is engaged in research in applied linguistics and the psychology of learning languages; the research team has begun work on two projects: firstly, applying programmed learning techniques to an audio-visual Spanish course for adult beginners, research into visual perception of meaning and the place and role of the visual element in such programmed courses; and, secondly, advanced French language learning for post A – level university students. This involves research in linguistics, psycho- and socio- linguistics, stylistics, testing, etc. to which other French departments are contributing, but the work is hampered by lack of recording facilities. In Birmingham University, van der Will is experimenting with tapes for class and private study as part of practical language work in German at an advanced level; at Newcastle, O'Callaghan has developed language laboratory exercises in pronunciation, grammar, comprehension and dialogue in Swedish for first-year university students; Barnett at Portsmouth College of Technology is using tapes for consecutive translation, remedial drills and for passages to be listened to and repeated while, at Cambridge, Fechner is using spaced tapes dividing the natural intonation of sentence patterns into smaller units. Du Feu (1968) discusses use of a language laboratory in teaching of minimal skills courses at East Anglia; it is used in teaching Russian, German and French for scientists, students of fine arts, history majors etc. Dickinson (1970) suggests use of tape to teach overseas students to understand spoken, conversational English. Information concerning other studies in progress is available from the Center for Information on Language Teaching and many techniques are reviewed in books by Healey (1967) and by Adam and Shawcross (1963).

Television is the only visual aid which can form a living link between different schools or different sections of the same school. Not only can very large audiences be reached simultaneously but experiences are accessible which could normally be observed by only one or two people at a time or in which the presence of even one observer could act as an interference. In medical schools, closed circuit television now enables large numbers of students to view an operation when it takes place or subsequently on video tape, to view a single specimen under the microscope or to observe a specialist's interview with his patient. At the Royal Free Hospital department of pathology, two such experiments have recently been made, one linking the school with the public mortuary, the other linking five schools in different parts of the country during a pathology seminar. In the first experiment (Special Correspondent, 1966 a) a large number of students were able to view in comfort and without loss of time in travelling; gross appearances were easily seen and the pathologist's comments were very helpful although details were possibly rather difficult to appreciate and lack of colour was a disadvantage. During the second experiment (Special Correspondent, 1966 b) two cases were discussed by pathologists in the hospital school, comments and questions being invited from the other Schools. This resulted in a lively discussion of one diagnosis which had obvious value in extending the knowledge of students and, conceivably, of some members of staff.

Dr. J. L. M. Trim reports that, in Cambridge, closed-circuit television is used in language teaching to enable teachers to conduct several classes simultaneously. This is achieved by using a monitor in each of 30 booths in the language laboratory. Bennet (1968) describes use of CCTV at Cambridge in teaching first-year students to read at a fairly fast pace while listening to a recording of the text. Closed-circuit television is also used in Glasgow and elsewhere to link Colleges of Education and schools so enabling students to observe classes in action with a minimum of interference from their observation. The most extensive experimental use of closed-circuit television has been in the Nine Universities Experiment. Authors of the report (Research Unit of the National Extension College, 1966a) comment:

> '.... the use of closed-circuit television in appropriate departments is rapidly becoming standard practice in British universities; ....the use of lectures and demonstrations recorded by one means or another is already well-established in some of them; .... there is a modest but increasing traffic between departments.' However, they find that, '.... the idea of creating a permanent network of links for the exchange of 'live' television material between a group of universities .... has serious administrative and financial drawbacks.... The exchange of recorded material at present offers an altogether more flexible way of pooling resources and from the technical point of view calls only for apparatus which will be equally valuable for intra-university purposes.'

Kallenbach and Gall (1969) found that the use of TV in micro-teaching saved time and expense, and was administratively more convenient, but no more effective. Harrington and Knoblett (1968) found CCTV less effective with business studies students but cheaper with more than 350 students. To overcome problems of staff shortage Robertson (1969) used video-tape recordings of modified conventional lectures in engineering. Information was written on cards displayed around the studio for ease of following them in a sequence with the camera.

Cowan, McConnell and Bolton (1970) substituted a carefully designed programme including CCTV, discussions, lecture notes, unstructured practical periods and 'open tutorials' for formal lectures and tutorials to achieve students objectives such as (1) lucid expression, (2) profitable independent technical reading, (3) answering and asking specific questions, and (4) accurate observation. The ratio of staff to student contact hours was $20\frac{1}{2}$: 1 compared with the UGC average ratio of 13.8 : 1, yet group interaction and staff-student contact were better than on the replaced lecture-tutorial system. Examinations showed more spontaneous syntheses of material from various subjects. They concluded that even with large classes the objectives and methods were feasible, efficient and attractive to students.

Professor Cherry comments on the value of video tape of a lecture for the purpose of revision, to clarify difficulties or to enable an absent student to catch up.

A catalogue of audio-visual activities in higher education (Research Unit of the National Extension College, 1966b) is available from the National Extension College.

Comparisons of teaching by television with traditional lectures or other conventional methods do not, at the present time, give a complete picture of their relative advantages. Maclaine (1965) describes an experiment at the University of Sydney in which postgraduate students of education attended lectures, listened to a lecture on television, or viewed a television demonstration, but no significant differences were found in the students' ability to recall information or to indicate how to apply it. The impersonality and pace of the TV lecture were criticized, the demonstration being considered more interesting.

On an immediate multiple-choice post-test Sclare and Thomson (1968) found that a group taught psychiatry by CCTV did significantly better than one taught by conventional case study demonstration, but no better than one taught by programmed instruction. But since the first two groups also showed a favourable change of attitude to the subject, CCTV appeared to be the most valuable of the three methods.

Using restricted technical equipment with students of electrical engineering, Craig (1968) obtained satisfactory results when prepared notes were issued immediately prior to transmission, and followed by tutorials; presentation was of a high standard, and the medium was not over-used.

Macfarlane Smith reports of students in 27 engineering science departments that those who included BBC programmes in a course did better in an objective test of knowledge and developed a more favourable attitude to the subject than students who followed the conventional courses (Macfarlane Smith, 1968). He later confirmed these findings, obtaining significant positive correlations between students' attainments in five engineering examinations and attitudes to their course, and between their examination and intelligence test scores. Students of above average intelligence, especially as measured by verbal tests, showed particular benefit from the programmes as compared with controls.

Experiments in English Medical Schools in teaching surgery by use of television (Smith and Wyllie, 1965; Smith et al., 1966) showed more benefit from television, particularly to the lower 85 per cent of students, and 29 out of 36 students who commented on the value of television as a teaching method approved it. The lecturers who use the method observe that students benefit more from TV when it is used as an ancillary visual aid, integrated into teaching, than if it is used as an unaccompanied visual aid.

Straightforward comparisons of TV with other teaching methods probably do not have much meaning. Instead, careful studies are required of how TV is used and what it is used for. Gibb (1968) tested the effectiveness of a commentary super-imposed over a video tape recording of a classroom situation shown to student-teachers. The commentary seemed essential to enable students to see the structure of the lesson but was less effective to demonstrate teaching techniques and the use of visual aids. Groups who heard the commentary could not apply what they had learned to a second lesson which immediately followed the first. This may be explained by fatigue since the differences in tests between those who heard the commentary, and controls, in the first lesson grew less significant for items occurring later in the lesson. Answers to specific questions suggest that viewers have a limited capacity to process incoming information and that they tend to ignore auditory information when both auditory and visual information are presented together. Gibb suggests that unless auditory material is compelling, cues taking 0.3 seconds, such as 'Notice that....' are needed to give the viewer time to switch to his auditory channel. In general it is wiser to give important verbal information when there is little visual competition. However, the work of Vernon (1953) and Trenaman (1967) indicates that, because visuals hold attention while the acquisition of information is consolidated by words, visual and auditory material should be closely integrated. Problems of fatigue and attention span have been considered by Wood and Hedley (1968), Barrington (1965) and Mills (1966). The general consensus seems to be that programmes should last for between 15 and 25 minutes.

We have previously mentioned the importance of feedback for the attention and recall of information. By using CCTV, James (1970) has shown its value in the learning of motor and inter-personal skills by apprentices, trampoliners, musical conductors and workers in the social sciences. Wood and Hedley (1968) and Perrott and Duthie (1969) have reported mixed reactions from student teachers viewing their performance in the classroom, weaker students being less favourable and more sensitive. Others (Hale, 1965) found it difficult to assess the general class atmosphere from TV. Mills (1966) and Wood and Hedley (1968) report improved understanding of teaching techniques from demonstrations but Mills, like Gibb (1968), found no significant improvement in their application to classroom situations. Hancock and Robinson (1966) report that a combination of CCTV and group discussion is stimulating for social workers.

Possibly the greatest contribution to efficiency in teaching is that of <u>film and film strip</u> for they can be sent to groups who lack teachers or be used for private study. However, the number of British experiments in connection with conventional teaching in higher education is small. An extensive, carefully designed investigation into teaching in the Royal Navy was made by Vernon, comparing classes taught with the aid of film or film strips (Vernon, 1946). Seven main types of instruction were used combining the methods in different ways. Closely comparable improvements in examinations, averaging about eight per cent, resulted from the use of the film-strip, from the addition of the film, from good versus poor instructors and from high versus low intelligence in the classes. Those improvements were highly significant statistically. The film was perhaps most successful since it took less time than the strip; when shown in conjunction with the strip it aided comprehension rather than memory for details. The film, or film strip, could largely compensate for weakness among instructors, but the taking of notes was of little value.

Kenshole (1968) prepared a film loop and a tape with slides to teach three-phase alternating current theory, in place of the usual six one hour lectures. This did not lead to any significant improvement in attainment by first year students but resulted in a significant saving of time of 40 per cent.

Ash and Carlton (1953), who studied the value of note-taking during film learning, found that it appeared to set up interference with viewing which was not wholly compensated for even when time was given to review notes subsequently.

The efficiency of film in conjunction with other methods has also been demonstrated in the teaching of physiology (Steinberg and Lewis, 1951). Showing of the film increased knowledge of both groups of students appreciably but was most effective after prolonged preparation; however, their teachers doubted whether the additional time spent in preparation was worthwhile.

No experiments have been traced with <u>film loops</u> or with <u>automatic slide projectors</u> although some interesting pieces of apparatus and related materials have been prepared for use in teaching. Film loops lasting two or three minutes each have to be devised to illustrate a succession of concepts, so enabling students to use them in any order or to select only those of special interest to them. In the case of the slide projector accompanied by tape, or written statements of what to observe, it would be interesting to know whether questions and subsequent answers would result in better retention of material than statements. Experience in programmed learning suggests that a challenge to the student to make a response, with immediate correction of his answer, would be far more effective than the relatively passive method of telling him what to look for.

The use of <u>computers</u> in British Higher Education is still in its early infancy. Flood Page (1970b) reports that 15 to 20 institutions of Higher Education are considering, or trying out, the use of computers for teaching purposes. The National Centre for Educational Technology (NCET) has made suggestions for the future direction of research. Dr. R.A. Wisbey has used a computer at Cambridge for the selection and grading of language materials. De Dombel, Hartley and Sleeman (1969) report the use of a computer to teach the techniques of clinical diagnosis to medical students. It can provide facts about a 'patient' and respond in answer to questions. When the student enters his diagnosis by teletype, the computer indicates any errors and invites the student to try again. The intention is to help students to see the significance of findings and guide them so that they proceed logically, eliciting information fully at each stage — an objective common to many subjects. Although it cannot teach skills with patients, the method seems to have the approval of students and to teach effectively. Harrison (1968) has described a number of developments such as a computer linked to a teaching machine in a mobile classroom. This can provide a record of each student's progress, modify instructions in accordance with an individual's previous responses, give continuous evaluation, and serve a large number of students simultaneously. Grubb (1968) presented a 'map' of a statistics course on a cathode ray tube to mature students. They chose which section they wished to tackle, and an IBM 1500 computer routed them through the course. Motivation was improved and a record of student choices could give information for the design of future courses. Other <u>electronic aids</u> are mentioned by Mr. J. Martin at the University of Kent at Canterbury where electronic equipment is used to increase reading effectiveness in foreign languages. At the Faculty of Technology in Manchester, electronic scanning gives access to library material at a distance.

SKILLS AND ABILITIES

A wide variety of skills and abilities are required in learning at the university level, ranging from mechanical and manual skills, in which one procedure must be learned and repeated accurately, to higher mental abilities, such as skill in solving unfamiliar problems, where flexibility in thinking and capacity to consider unexpected possibilities play a considerable part in success. Different methods of learning and teaching are required in these cases but an essential in learning all skills is that the student should have adequate opportunity for practice and should receive information as to his success.

Mechanical and Manual Skills

Learning of mechanical and manual skills has not been studied experimentally among university students although there are a number of interesting innovations in teaching.

In industry, however, fairly extensive studies have been made in the teaching and learning of skills. Many of these are described by Seymour (1966). Some of the findings have relevance to practical skills learned in certain university courses such as the filling of a tooth, dissection of a cadaver or assembly of electrical circuits from diagrams. Seymour distinguishes the 'knowledge' and 'skills' content in learning a practical task. The former involves memory for symbolic material in the form of words, numbers or diagrams, which is said to be learned when it has been memorized and can be recalled appropriately; the skills content involves non-symbolic information and its acquisition requires motor and perceptual learning. If the knowledge content can be readily memorized, the control of the motor activities can proceed unimpeded. Difficulty arises when diagrams and written texts have to be consulted as the task proceeds or where the level of discrimination required is near the threshold for that particular sense. This difficulty is overcome in learning skills, such as dissections, where instructions are played on audio-tape which the student can stop at will. Alternatively, a tape dealing with the entire process, emphasizing difficult points, seems highly effective. In a personal communication, Dr. Goodhue of the Biology Department at Trinity College, Dublin reports that tapes, together with diagrams and other illustrations he has prepared, have proved so successful in teaching first-year students to dissect rats that their initial attempt which formerly took three hours, with many errors (after a demonstration) are now completed almost perfectly in one hour.

Experiments suggest that it is wasteful to practice too intensively initially. Henshaw et al., (1933) did an experiment with three groups of 30 subjects employed on chain assembly for 80 minutes each morning. In the afternoon, Group I did another 80 minutes chain assembly, Group II practised a different operation and Group III did no assembly, yet the performance of the three groups remained almost identical; but it is a common experience that rest periods improve performance – in learning to drive a car, for instance, or in learning to swim. Seymour suggests that the optimum period of practice initially is half an hour, extending to two hours when the individual is already practised.

An observation in many of the more complex skills is that the learner reaches plateaux, where he appears to make little or no progress, but that these are followed by rapid improvements, possibly owing to the synthesis of a number of skills. Whether the skill transfers to another task seems to follow from the extent to which it depends on selecting similar groupings of activities of the muscles, and the skill the individual shows in 'selectivity' i.e. in more frequent selection of optimum responses. Of interest here is a finding that in learning to type, students who began to learn on an electric typewriter later attained greater speeds on a manual typewriter than those who learned to use the manual typewriter first. Thus initial 'pacing' by the machine had a lasting effect (Garbutt, 1963).

Contradictory results have been obtained in studies of learning by part or whole methods. Woodworth (Seymour, 1966) favoured the 'whole' method with special attention to and repetition of difficult or important parts. This may account for Goodhue's success since his method consists in showing the whole dissection, but with coloured diagrams for critical stages. Experiments at Birmingham University Department of Engineering Production (Seymour, 1966, Ch. 8) suggests that a more useful distinction is between perceptual content of different parts of the task than between 'part' and 'whole'. Results of one experiment suggest that elements of a task with difficult perceptual content require longer training and that, therefore, methods which enable greater attention to be concentrated on these are advantageous.

As in other fields, knowledge of results leads to more rapid learning; what is needed is an exact and prompt indication of what went wrong and the direction from 'wrong' to 'right'.

Study Skills

The term 'study skills' is used here to cover all such skills as speed and comprehension in reading, note-taking or methods of learning from notes and books; thus, they are essentially verbal skills but do not include oral skills, verbal fluency or literary style. In the university there has been a tendency to take such skills for granted; exceptional slowness in reading may be remarked on but it is not usually thought of as remediable; it is rare to find a university teacher who makes a point of exploring his students' method of study and guiding them to use more effective techniques, yet the few investigations which have so far been made suggest that this is one area in which considerable advances could still be achieved.

Malleson et al. (1968) inquired into methods of study of medical students, asking them to record for each session of study a number one to eight corresponding with eight different methods. They also investigated a number of attitudes and were able, tentatively, to identify certain factors in study e.g. (1) syllabus oriented: pressured v. easy going, (2) methodical v. enjoyable, (3) self-confident v. anxious.

Comparatively recently, attention has been given to speed and comprehension in reading and to the possibility of teaching students or adults to skim in reading. Barclay used films specially prepared to increase reading speeds with 61 graduate students drawn from various professions, in an attempt to see whether reading speed could be increased while at least maintaining the level of comprehension (Barclay, 1957). All students made increases in reading speed, ranging from seven to 213 per cent, and averaging 81 per cent. An overall improvement in comprehension was also remarked and, after lectures on methods of skimming and scanning, the group achieved a substantial cut in time taken to find facts. Although this and the succeeding experiments are encouraging, there is probably need for more extensive experiments to determine to what extent the skill is retained and whether it applies only with materials similar to those used in the initial experiment. If this proves to be so, further experiments should be undertaken using more varied materials in training the students.

Hill and Scheuer (1965) used a rapid reading course for medical students, prepared by Fry (1963 a, 1963 b) with 13 senior pathology students. In their case reading speed increased on the average by 110 per cent, individual improvement ranging from 36 to 241 per cent. Comprehension level was slightly raised and satisfactory speeds were reached in skimming following an exercise in the middle of the course.

A summary of many similar investigations undertaken among eight experimental populations has been made by Poulton (1961). In the 66 groups who took part in such experiments, mean gains in reading speed ranged from 11 to 148 per cent while those in comprehension lay between -20 and +89 per cent. In cases where performance was re-tested some time after the experiment, individuals differed considerably in their capacity to maintain gains, some deteriorating almost to previous levels whereas others almost entirely maintained their new high levels.

Following a review of recent literature, Wright (1968) suggests that efficient reading involves three stages: a pre-view which is often achieved by skimming, fast reading of the passage, and a review. She quotes Alderman (1926) who found that exercises designed to increase the reader's ability to organize what he read resulted in greater improvement in a comprehension test than exercises intended either to develop vocabulary or to increase retention. She considers that the most important characteristic of written information is its structure and that the reader must restructure difficult material to provide his own 'cognitive map'.

Another investigation of interest, because it should lead to greater understanding of how students study and so lead to better means of guiding them, is that of Jahoda and Thomas (1966). They are in the process of finding out in what ways students and lecturers set about extracting information from books and lectures and how they define the learning task to themselves. In a pilot survey, 20 individuals were asked to study each of three passages – an introduction to cybernetics presenting a rigorously logical argument; a history text requiring memory for relatively unfamiliar names and a text on clinical psychology in common sense terms – until they felt they had learned it; they were then asked to compose questions which would adequately test whether a person had learned the passage and were themselves asked questions designed to test what they had learned and at what level of abstraction. During the course of study their progress from page to page was recorded. It proved that techniques differed widely: rapid scanning followed by study of selected passages, perhaps repeatedly, a careful first reading checking back only on a few important passages, constant referral to earlier paragraphs, and so on. Some used identical strategies on each passage whereas others generated strategies appropriate to the material. Questions set by members of the experimental sample in some cases dealt wholly with details while others concentrated on principles. As a result of this pilot study alone, the authors consider that staff time spent early in a course on individual tutoring, encouraging students to examine their learning processes, could save time later and increase the students' range.

Freyberg has experimented with several methods of note-taking (Freyberg, 1956) but these were imposed by the experimenter. He used four methods with parallel groups of students: taking no notes, writing full notes, making an outline or accepting a duplicated summary. His findings suggest that these methods are effective for different purposes: where material was to be recalled very soon but was not required for examinations, taking no notes proved most successful; if it was to be examined, learning from duplicated notes gave the best results. However, the experiment is a limited one. Further experiments would be required to show how these different methods influenced students' learning and study skills over a longer period, and prior discussion with some students of how to take notes more effectively might substantially influence results if the experiment was repeated.

Hartley and Cameron (1967) investigated note taking by recording the number of items in a lecture and checking how many of these were mentioned by students in notes. Rather less than one third of what was said was transmitted to note books but this included about half of what the lecturer considered important. References, definitions, names and words written on the blackboard were recorded but experiments leading to theory were omitted. The method suggested that the students regarded the lecture as a framework of ideas and theory in which to fit subsequent work; all reported that they would do subsequent work but only three of 22 students did any. The authors conclude that a weakness of the lecture system as a teaching method lies in the discrepancy between the students' stated and achieved objectives; they suggest that the lecturer should reconsider his own objectives, possible ways of attaining them and techniques to measure their achievement.

Ability to collect, collate and to apply information skilfully increases in importance with the rapid growth of knowledge and in number of specialities. It is an essential component in the capacity to respond flexibly to change. Since it tends to be taken for granted by those teachers who unthinkingly repeat courses and methods used by their teachers in more stable times, too many students are provided with almost all the information they need in lectures; they therefore have little incentive to develop this skill. Yet they need not only to learn to use libraries effectively but also to use modern techniques which will be more common during their professional lives, such as tape and slide sequences or computers. Fortunately there is a well established trend to increase activities which put the onus on students to collect information for themselves. Research projects are set to a growing number of undergraduates and these and long essays take the place of some traditional examination papers. Librarians are often invited to advise students on the use of library facilities;

but only one librarian has reported use of exercises and subsequent evaluation of their effects, during a short course designed to ensure that students gained skill in searching literature (Crossley, 1968). This resulted in a higher level of library inquiry and increased use of inter-library services. Wood (1969) also mentions exercises during a course of a similar kind.

Essay writing and the writing of laboratory reports are other skills which tend to be taken for granted by university teachers. One lecturer in London University mentioned recently how poor the essays were in the final examination of his department but, in reply to a question, he admitted that the students were not required to write a single essay during their three-year course! Evidently their teachers were making two assumptions, both of which we would consider unjustified: firstly, that students would have the skill to write essays despite lack of practice and, secondly, that answers in essay form were appropriate to test understanding or skill, in a subject which did not require verbal work of this kind while learning it. But this may be a common error: Beard, Levy and Maddox noted a high correlation between scores in a verbal test and an engineering drawing examination and commented that the examination was probably unnecessarily verbal in content (Beard et al., 1964).

Inquiry suggests that the amount of feedback students receive on writing varies enormously. Although it is obviously the intention in the old, and some new, universities that tutorials should fulfil this function, complaints by students indicate that this is not apparent to all tutors as some spend the time in giving a mini-lecture instead of initiating discussion about students' work. In London, where staffing does not usually permit individual tutorials, group discussion of essays is used in a number of departments, notably geography. Often a student is asked to read his essay to the group who then comment on structure, handling of material and use of illustrations, and so on. This seems to work well; but the practice of giving only literal grades has little to recommend it. At an SRHE conference in April 1970, one lecturer recalled having received the mark C++ to B-- for an essay he wrote as a student! His own practice as a tutor in a department of education is to list, first what he wishes to praise and, secondly, anything which he considers could be improved. The standard of students treated in this way steadily rose, whereas students who received only literal grades made no improvement.

Where written reports are required there is evidence that students can be helped to improve them considerably in the course of learning. Dr. A.P. Prosser (Imperial College, University of London) sets experimental problems to pairs of first-year engineering students who must solve the problem and discuss their solutions in some detail with the tutor before writing their reports (Prosser, 1967). He comments that the reports are technically of higher quality and more comprehensive since the introduction of this method, and that marked improvement can be observed during the year in describing and interpreting results. Although it is fairly generally agreed that putting one's ideas on paper is an aid to clarity in thinking, the ways in which it does so have not been investigated. It is almost certainly partly because inter-relationships too complex to hold in mind can be seen more readily when spelled out or arranged diagrammatically, but no doubt the effort to find the right word to express a half-framed idea in itself leads to greater clarity. Since it is one of the most important skills it deserves investigation, both as to how different individuals set about it and how teachers can aid students in improving their techniques.

Oral Skills and Group Discussion

Oral skills have always been important in the medical and dental professions for the doctor or dentist must communicate with his colleagues or with his patients; in the legal profession also, oral skills have always been an essential requirement to elicit information or to exercise persuasion. But, mainly since the war, proliferation of committees has increased the need for oral skills among engineers and scientists, while the use of television and other audio-visual aids has increased the use of oral communication and at the same time made audiences more critical. Consequently, not only must the student develop a capacity to present a report, or to engage in a discussion with experts in other fields but, as in all communication, he must appreciate factors which influence decisions, such as interaction between members of a committee, their difficulties with subject matter, any prejudices they are likely to show, and so on. So, for effective presentation of his case, the young scientist like the doctor or lawyer must learn to express himself well and should gain at least practical experience, if not theoretical knowledge, of group dynamics.

During the last few years, partly owing to the influence of the Hale Report, the use of group discussion methods has considerably increased in university teaching. Their chief purpose differs from subject to subject; thus, in biology, probably their most important purpose is encouragement of critical thinking, in mathematics, discussion of students' difficulties and, in engineering, younger students discuss problems primarily mathematical in nature whereas older ones are more likely to consider applications of engineering to industry (Beard, 1967a). But in most subjects at some time, there are occasions when a student gives a talk on a prepared topic and leads the subsequent discussion. In this way students may learn to play different roles within a group.

That even limited group discussion can have an influence on subsequent oral work was shown by Erskine and Tomkin (1963). After only two periods of discussion during a three-week course on anatomy, their students did appre-ciably better in oral examinations than those who attended nine lectures. Discussion is also one of the valuable features of group projects such as those described by physicists in Birmingham (Black, et al. 1968) or in engineering (Cowan et al. 1970). At Strathclyde (Douglas, 1970) students' performance is assessed when they lead engineering seminars which replace some laboratory periods.

The majority of studies of group interactions and of group discussion have been made in the United States; but there is a growing volume of contributions from British authors. Klein is the author of two books (1961, 1965); Sprott, (1958) surveys many studies both British and American; Abercrombie in The Anatomy of Judgement (1958) discusses factors which influence judgement and accuracy of observation. In Aims and Techniques of Group Teaching (1970) she relates group methods with objectives and outlines a series of meetings planned to help students to come to terms with the problems of changing status in the authority-dependency relationship. Some of this work will be discussed further in the section on teaching for change of attitudes; but here we are concerned with group dynamics independent objectives in teaching. There is general agreement that some of the important variables are seating position, talkativeness, personality of the participants and the kind of leadership. Position proves to be more important than casual observation suggests: the leader's position if he sits separate from the group but facing them, indicates that he expects members of the group to address him but not each other; if he sits at the head of a table this suggests that he expects to be addressed a substantial part of the time; he must sit among the group as a member of it, or outside it as an observer, if he wishes the group members usually to address each other. Individuals within the group tend to choose positions according to whether they wish to talk or not, preferring a place opposite the leader if they wish to talk to him, but adjacent to him otherwise; a member opposed to the group may withdraw his chair from the circle. Generally, members tend to address those who face them more than members placed adjacent to them. A teacher may use this to encourage a quiet member to talk by placing him opposite a talkative one, or quieten the talkative by placing them next to each other or to the leader. Persistently silent members must be assigned an active part by preparing a paper, or a few points to begin the discussion, while the over-talkative can be silenced by inviting him to be group secretary or by thanking him for his contribution and inviting other comments on the points he has raised.

Klein (1965) observed that in a series of free discussions members tended to establish characteristic interaction frequencies, high interactive sub-groups, particularly pairs, being formed. In line with American findings she found that the more voluble members tended to be popular and that agreement on the ranks of members increased as the series proceeded. American studies have shown also that it is the talkative members who can most readily get the support of the group. A normally silent member given the best solution of a problem fails to get it accepted without the aid of one of the most voluble participants. Tuckman and Lorge also found (Tuckman and Lorge, 1962) that contributions by members of low status were normally ignored in arriving at a group solution to a problem; in such a case the solution arrived at by putting together the best points from all individual solutions excelled the solution of the same individuals when working in a group.

Deutsch studied the effect of giving different information to group members as to the assessment of group work (Deutsch, 1949). Some groups were told that they would be assessed collectively, in co-operation, while others were informed that each individual would be assessed independently, in competition with other members of the group. The 'co-operative' group showed more co-ordination of effort, diversity in amount of contribution, sub-division of activity, attentiveness to fellow members, mutual comprehension and communication, greater orientation and orderliness and productivity per unit time, as well as favourable evaluation of the group and its products. Berkowitz et al. found (1957) that, in groups of three students who were evaluated favourably or unfavourably for contribution made, those groups in which all members were unfavourably rated were most integrated and most highly motivated, while those in which members received different ratings found each other less attractive and were least motivated.

Thus, in both cases, an element of competition and perceived difference in achievement were destructive of a group spirit and achievement within the group. Personality may also have a similar effect; Haythorn et al. found (1956) that students of a markedly authoritarian personality were more aggressive and less effective in group discussion than those who were rated 'egalitarian' on the California F-scale.

Contributions of a discussion leader as compared with an observer have been studied by Maier and Solem (1952). They found that minorities obtained a better hearing in a group having a leader and tended to be sheltered by the leader, so that minorities with strongly expressed, but wrong, views continued to hold them in groups with a leader. but were forced to change their views and to accept a correct solution in leaderless groups. This suggests that free group discussion with an observer may be more effective in encouraging critical thinking than discussion in a group with a teacher; but the scope of the experiment is inadequate for anything more than a suggestion that this may be worth investigating further. In an experiment with 800 groups of different sizes Davey (1969) concluded that a permissive style of leadership was most productive with groups having four to seven members, but that a controlling style was more effective for fewer than four or more than seven.

The value of discussion between students in the absence of a lecturer does not appear to be recognized generally in university courses. Students consulted by Marris (1965) said that they frequently discussed their work with each other and could be less inhibited with staff absent; it was a more satisfactory way of dealing with difficulties since they felt that seeking help from staff was viewed as a confession of incompetence. Teachers who have organized work so that students discussed questions together in pairs, or small groups, before raising further questions with them have found the method very successful (Beard, 1967 b).

Higher Mental Skills

Critical thinking

'Critical thinking', 'scientific thinking' or 'understanding' are terms which come readily to the minds of teachers when they are asked to outline their chief aims in teaching. However, it is commonly added that many students are very limited in their capacity to think critically. Medical students are often mentioned as a group 'less able than most honours students' who, due to poor ability, are dependent on their teachers, unable to learn without considerable guidance and who, moreover, must be enabled to recall a mass of information before it is possible for them to begin to discuss intelligently or to deal with problems. Teachers who argue in this way would do well to study the findings of psychologists who have investigated the factors operating in transfer of training.

Thorndike (1913) in the earlier phases of these investigations concluded that only identical elements of content, or pattern of procedure, could be transferred from one learning situation to another. In the case of medical courses, for example, some procedures in pre-clinical subjects are relevant in related post-clinical work and to this extent habits of work transfer directly and beneficially. But transfer applies equally to undesirable habits: learning by rote without understanding, accepting rather than challenging authoritarian statements and concentrating on accumulation of facts rather than interpreting them or making decisions, are also likely to be transferred to the post-clinical course if they have been the pattern of behaviour in the pre-clinical school. Since recent work suggests that more generalized training may be transferred when there is similarity between the new situation and the one in which the behaviour was learned, it seems imperative to provide a situation in which students are encouraged to be critical as soon as possible. Thus teachers who insist that medical knowledge can be introduced by means of problems which require initiative and understanding in the students as they solve them are more likely to train doctors of a critical habit of mind with capacity to educate themselves.

A useful concept is that of 'sets' which consist of expectations based on past experience. In an experiment in the psychology laboratory students attempt to obtain stated quantities of liquid from combinations of three given amounts. The first four problems can be solved only by subtracting the second from the first and adding the third. The fifth problem can be solved in this way but also, more easily, by simply subtracting the third from the first amount. By no means all of those who attempt the problems see the easy alternative. They have developed a 'set' which is useful while conditions remain the same but which is inhibiting so soon as they change. Individuals differ in their flexibility in situations of this kind; those who normally welcome ambiguity and novelty being more likely to hit on the more economical solution. Teachers can use methods which develop flexibility in thinking by fostering 'sets' of a constructive kind, for instance, by teaching strategies for attacking problems rather than, or in addition to, 'sets' for specific types of solution.

A constructive use of 'set' is made in teaching French literature in one department of London University (Uren, 1968). A preliminary discussion takes place around the theme of the text to be studied, and students are asked to predict points that the author has made. It is not common for students to bring up in this way all the points touched on in the text before they have even heard it. They are encouraged by their own display of knowledge and listen to the text very attentively to see how it treats the theme. Their tutor takes the opportunity to point out the value of their adopting a similar strategy in their personal reading.

Psychologists would also expect students, like children, to succeed best where teaching methods arouse most interest and most activity on the part of the learner. With children evidence already exists that retention of information is at least as good when it is gained as a by-product of solving problems as when inculcated by efficient teaching of information only. No doubt this is partly because the information becomes organized into a meaningful whole which, as we have seen, aids retention. Further, the method is likely to inspire so much interest that the children spontaneously follow up the problems, thus extending their range of learning. However, we cannot say categorically that teaching students through problems is more efficient than other current methods, in terms of inculcation of information, for no experiment has been carried out at their level comparing this method with others.

That there is an essential difficulty in thinking objectively, owing to unconscious assumptions and habits built up in the course of learning, has been shown by

Abercrombie and others; reception of information, recollections, observations and description, judgements or inferences are alike affected. These assumptions operate even with relatively simple material in visual illusions, in giving verbal definitions or in understanding the meaning of a word, as well as in tasks for which more training is needed such as interpreting X-rays. Teachers have various methods of combating this problem but it is questionable whether they are fully aware of its extent. They recognize that for the student to be led to new skills for which his existing habits and skills are inadequate they must organize new material in a way which is meaningful to him. But if the step is too great for him, or a problem too difficult, they tend to repeat their first explanation or to show again the steps of a solution to the problem without examining the student's assumptions and preconceptions. To do so involves either prior study of all possible wrong assumptions, with questions or procedures to correct them (as provided in some branching programmed texts) or discussion.

Johnson-Abercrombie experimented with undirected group discussions. Her aim was to avoid instruction in a 'correct' method but to develop a scientific method by stimulating students to work out problems among themselves by mutual questioning and correction. For example, in an early study with James and Venning, one group of students was trained to be observant in studying X-rays and other visual material by criticism of their own descriptions and inferences, so becoming aware of assumptions and preconceptions which influenced the receipt of visual information (James et al. 1956). It should be noted that the experimenter did not play the part of a director of discussion but was an onlooker who asked a question or commented somewhat in the manner of a psychiatrist in a group therapy session. The responses of the participants are also reminiscent of volunteers or patients in group therapy. Some inquired the purpose of it all and asserted that they had gained nothing from such undirected work (rejecting the experience), while others developed feelings of insecurity or hostility which they worked through; and nearly all were astonished, or even dismayed, on discovering how greatly unconscious assumptions had influenced their judgements. In subsequent comparison of this group with one conventionally taught, in observation of three X-rays, the trained group were superior to a highly significant degree: they made fewer false inferences, fewer inferences unaccompanied by descriptions, more of them considered two hypotheses rather than one only and a smaller number were inappropriately biased by one test in dealing with the succeeding one. Evidently a change in behaviour did occur due to this kind of general discussion. Barnett (1958) used group discussion in a similar fashion with eight students using alternate two-hour meetings, in a series of 24, for free discussion following the reading of a brief, and sometimes controversial, passage or article; like Abercrombie, he observed the discussions without intervening until the end. He found that students came gradually to stick more to the point and to criticize each other's arguments more effectively — there was rather less arbitrary statement of personal prejudices and rather more attempt at rational argument, but these trends were only beginning to appear towards the end of 12 periods of discussion. Behaviour of some members of the group was noticeably influenced, e.g. in talking more, or less, or in becoming less aggressive.

What evidence there is suggests that lectures do not exert a comparable influence on students to make them think more critically, but only one study (other than that of Abercrombie) is British. Elton (1965) compared students following courses of logic instruction and applied psychology in their capacity to reason, as measured by Valentine's Reasoning Test, before and after their courses. Although the philosophy class studied a 16 week course devoted to the logical principles underlying valid thought they made no greater improvement in scores than did the students of psychology. A promising line of investigation is suggested by Garbutt (1963) who collected text book definitions of terms used in accountancy. There were ten distinct definitions of 'capital'. When students were asked to define words commonly used in their first term's study many poor definitions, or none, were given of some of them, 'capital' proving the most difficult. It seems probable that, in a number of subjects, students cannot be intelligently critical because they simply do not know what they are talking about.

In surveying barriers to progress among students of social psychology, Gibson (1970) lists six main kinds of error: first, the notion that theories and hypotheses have been falsified when they have been shown not to apply in certain circumstances; second, over-generalization of experimental results; third, failure to recognize particular experiments as building blocks in a wider theory so that when experimental results cannot immediately be extrapolated to society at large, they are regarded as useless; fourth, lack of knowledge of research which would give precise meaning to terms such as 'balance', 'attitude' or 'prejudice'; fifth, rejection complete or partial, of quantitative data in the belief that essential aspects of the subject must be missed if quantitative data are insisted on; and, sixth, confusion over what constitutes evidence. Thus he cites, in more detail, the kinds of complaints made by Abercrombie of biology students in the 1950's. The evidence, to date at least, is that her remedy may be the most effective.

Researchers in America also suggest that discussion plays an important part in the development of critical thinking (1966). It is of interest, too, that the extensive and careful observations and experiments made by Inhelder and Piaget into the development of children's thinking have led to similar conclusions (Inhelder and Piaget, 1958). Piaget believes that the final stage, normally achieved in adolescence, in which children learn to accept assumptions and hypotheses from which they make deductions, develops primarily as a result of appreciating different view-points in discussion and co-operation. Indeed, in the absence of co-operation and the resulting discussion, he believes that this final level of thinking fails to develop for, he says .... 'the coercions of other people would not be enough to engender a logic in the child's mind, even if the truths that they imposed were rational in content; repeating correct ideas, even if one believes that they originate from oneself, is not the same as reasoning correctly. On the contrary, in order to teach others to reason logically it is indispensable that there should be established between them and oneself those simultaneous relationships of differentiation and reciprocity which characterize the co-ordination of viewpoints.' Since the majority of students do not reason consistently logically there appears to be sufficient evidence here for extensive use of discussion between students or, as nearly as possible on a basis of equality, between teacher and students.

Making diagnoses or decisions and solving familiar problems

Despite the importance of problem solving and decision making in university work there is no systematic body of inquiry into processes of learning these skills nor, until recently, any analysis of them with a view to more effective teaching. But analysis of subject matter by teachers and psychologists engaged in writing programmed books, or programmes for teaching machines, and that by psychologists preparing 'flow-charts' of instructions enabling the reader to arrive at decisions by means of simple alternative choices, have indicated new approaches in teaching.

Gane, Horabin and Lewis (1966) have begun work on clarifying decision-making in industry and in government directives to the public, but they have also suggested application in other topics including the making of diagnoses in medicine. They give an example for the diagnosis of Reynaud's Disease and Secondary Reynaud's Phenomenon, too complex to reproduce here; but a simple example (sketched on the following page) suffices to demonstrate the method although it does not require the cross linking and diversity of possible solutions of the medical diagnosis chart.

By this technique, everything which must be taken into account is itemized. Different methods of presenting the data can avoid production of excessively large charts, either by listing instructions or by presenting a number of sub-charts. The use of charts of these kinds in industry has resulted in dramatic improvements in training time and in general efficiency. Their value in university teaching has not yet been explored, but the authors suggest that medical diagnosis charts may be used to update experienced practitioners with new developments or as useful memory 'joggers'. They have an obvious value to the advanced student in giving him, almost at one glance, all the factors which need to be taken into account in coming to a decision. The authors comment that the same advantages would hold if the chart dealt with completely different kinds of subject matter such as, say, technological information or the laws relating to taxation. Almost certainly somewhat similar charts would guide students in the solution of familiar kinds of mathematical problems.

Designers of programmed books have analyzed subject matter and strategies in solving problems to present them in such a way that specific methods of problem-solving are learned and more general problem solving techniques are derived. One essential factor in successful solution appears to be recall, or reminder, of relevant principles. Where a reminder is needed it has been found more effective not to state the required principles but to ask questions which result in the student recalling or rediscovering them.

A technique increasingly used in America and beginning to be used in Britain is the 'simulation technique'. Tests or 'games' are used to simulate situations in which it would be unsafe or impracticable for students to take charge in reality, such as diagnosing and treating diseases, deciding on land uses, replanning a town, and so on (Taylor and Carter, 1967; Taylor and Maddison, 1967). In this

BOILER WATER ANALYSIS ACTION GUIDE

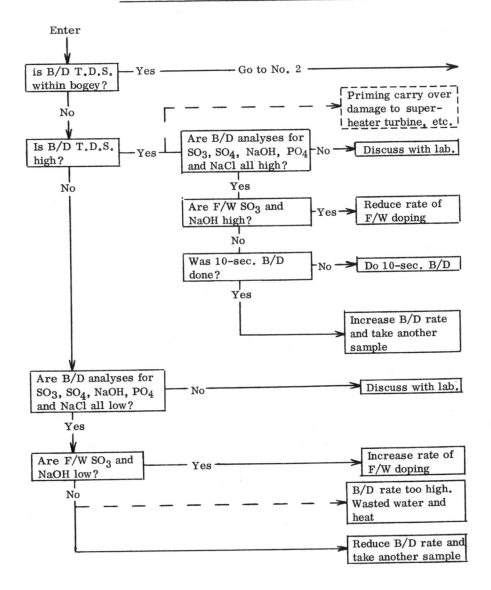

way the medical student, for example, can decide on tests and treatments, selecting as many as he wishes from a list provided, following through the consequences of his decisions in subsequent sections of a booklet until his 'patient' recovers or succumbs. This may be a useful supplement to observations on the wards; some students who have used the method commented that they realized for the first time the consequences of the decisions they would be called on to make (McCarthy and Gonella, 1967). A recent book by British authors (Armstrong and Taylor, 1970) describes instructional simulation systems for use in higher education in military studies, management training, teaching of industrial relations, urban and regional studies, international relations, local government and for development of social skills. Although their effectiveness is discussed, systematic evaluation of these methods has not been undertaken; they are used and valued because they partly supply the need to study consequences of alternative courses of action and interactions between groups having conflicting interests. A game to teach skills in business is described by Hargreaves (1970). The method has also been applied in teacher training by Tansey (1969) who provided case studies requiring decisions by 'teachers'. He points out the advantages of involving students in situations without risk which sensitize them to the real world of teaching, bringing together theory and practice in education.

Solving unfamiliar problems, creative thinking

Ability to solve unfamiliar problems is becoming increasingly important in scientific work, but there has been practically no systematic study of this skill. A recent study by Connor of students' problem-solving identified several stages in solving moderately familiar problems; but the students proved very poor at unfamiliar tasks and it was rare for them to check on adequacy or appropriateness of their conclusions (Connor, 1967). There seems to be a fairly prevalent belief that inventive and creative workers are born, not made, despite evidence that some university departments and certain teachers have produced an unexpectedly high number of creative workers. There is evidence too that the greater proportions of distinguished scientific workers in America came from the Eastern coast initially but subsequently have been produced by schools further and further west. These findings at least suggest that creative talent is a product of inborn ability with favourable early experience maybe, but also inspired teaching or example at university level. Since good success in first-degree courses does not necessarily indicate capacity for original work nor a poor degree inability to think creatively, there is some evidence that existing first-degree examinations and courses fail to give sufficient opportunity to students to solve unfamiliar problems or to show originality. Hudson (1966) observed that in Cambridge there was no relation between degree class and subsequent academic honours: fully a third of the future FRS's at Cambridge had gained a second or worse at some time during their university careers and the proportion among future D.Sc.'s was over a half. In an investigation in the Geography Department at Newcastle, undergraduates who did well in traditional examinations performed at least competently in research but those who excelled in research projects did not necessarily perform well in examinations; less than half of them gained examination marks as high as B+ (Whiteland, 1966). In consequence there is a move in some departments to take account of dissertations or other original course work for the final assessment. Although ability to think creatively is increasingly required, no British investigation into teaching methods to encourage it has been traced; nevertheless there are many innovations in teaching. In both pure and applied sciences research projects and open-ended experiments for undergraduates are becoming fairly common.

Projects and problems

In 1965, Jones (1969) alone reported the use of carefully chosen projects in organic chemistry with third year students. The subject was chosen at the end of the Autumn Term; practical work was undertaken the following Spring and the paper produced at the end of the term contributed to the students' final assessments. Students worked jointly on a project or two or three students worked on related projects. This experiment was considered so successful that it was to become the standard third and fourth year course in practical organic chemistry. In engineering, projects were already employed by the middle of the last decade and a wide variety is now in use. Allen (1968) and Jeffries and Leech (1969) describe 'design and make' projects in which students prepare a design to the customer's specification, within an agreed budget and time. Coekin's students work in groups and cost the manufacture of production circuitry (1970). A different kind of project leads students to relate engineering studies with those in humanities and social sciences. A popular topic at Imperial College in 1967 required specific recommendations by the students of, say, a suitable product for an engineering firm to manufacture in a named developing country (Beard, 1967). A few students are able to pursue such topics overseas during summer vacations (Goodlad, 1970).

In an electrical machine laboratory, students choose their own projects (Holmes, 1969). At Heriot Watt University two different approaches are used (Cowan, et al. 1970). First year students have recently designed balsawood cantilever frames to support a loading bar some distance from a plane surface. They were fabricated to detailed drawings produced by groups in engineering drawing classes, and were tested to destruction in specially prepared rigs in the CCTV studio, students being asked to predict their modes of failure. These experiments aroused great enthusiasm which led in many cases to further inquiries. During the second year students select a topic for a project from a tentative list of suggestions and are expected to take charge of its development depending on their tutors for guidance only. In these there is considerable display of enthusiasm, intelligence and initiative – provided that staff do not direct too closely. It is of interest that assessments in projects show no correlation with exams.

A number of physicists describe projects which provide undergraduate students with opportunities to attempt unsolved problems and to study a subject in depth (Black et al. 1968; Elton et al. 1970; Foulds et al. 1969; Wooding, 1968). Wooding lists topics which have been found suitable and outlines the development of several in more detail. He and his colleagues have found that they must not work out the project very far before the student tackles it, or he tends to be guided too closely by the demonstrators. Alternative topics are available if a student proves to be attempting a problem which is too difficult for him.

Black and his colleagues (1968) find that their students contrast a feeling of 'sorting things out and learning' from projects with one of 'knowing nothing' as a result of cramming for finals in the rest of the course. Projects are also being employed with notable success in mathematics (Hirst and Biggs, 1969) and in medicine (Edwards, 1967; Hayes, 1964; Wright, E.A., 1968).

In courses where undergraduates lack the incentive, or ability, to undertake original work, and in arts subjects, dissertations are set which require mainly collection, collation and appraisal of published material. These are common in Colleges of Education and in some Technical Colleges and are increasingly set in university departments. Similar approaches are used in social sciences. Collier (1966, 1969) uses syndicates of five or six post-graduate students who work at group assignments in educational sociology. In addition to greater involvement and satisfaction, the method leads to more cogent reporting and allows greater independence than do traditional lectures with tutorials.

In colleges of art and education reporting to the NUS over half the students were working on a dissertation, thesis or project but only about one in eight of students in technical colleges and universities. The figure was particularly low in the two universities where three quarters of the students were neither told about, nor involved in, their departmental research. Yet it is usually assumed that the universities train the researchers of the future.

Teachers who hesitate to introduce projects often give as reasons that suitable topics and apparatus are difficult to supply or that assessment presents too serious problems. They find, for example, that tutors supply widely differing amounts of help, that work in groups makes individual contributions difficult to assess, and that since students tackle different topics there seems to be no adequate basis for comparison. Whilst there is some truth in this, the growing volume of suggestions for suitable topics may soon meet the first difficulty. The others present a challenge to improve methods of assessment rather than an excuse for ignoring an important aspect of students' work. Physicists at Queen Mary College, for instance, use independent interviews to assess group projects and set at least three intermediate half hour tests containing questions on principles and on the individual's area of contribution.

In Sussex, (Hirst and Biggs, 1969) the mathematicians have devised a common form of assessment for projects under four headings:

A	Exposition:	mathematical accuracy, clarity, literary presentation.
B	Literature:	understanding, relating different sources, finding new sources.
C	Originality:	examples cited, examples constructed, new treatments and proofs of standard results, simple generalizations, original researches.
D	Scope of topic:	conceptual difficulty, technical difficulty, relationship with previous studies, relevance of material included, coverage of the topic.

An extensive study of marking of A-level biology projects in which teachers and external moderators were given instructions about marking procedures resulted in satisfactory performance overall; but difficulties are discussed (Eggleston and Kelly, 1970).

As one would expect, evidence suggests that opportunity to work creatively results in a greater output of creative work. Hayes (1964) investigated the effect of student dissertations as part of a graduate requirement in medical school; during the three years of the experiment student participation in research increased: in 1961, 25 per cent, in 1962, 26.5 per cent and in 1963, 45.5 per cent of papers in the students' journal were based on original work. E.A. Wright (1968) also reports that an increasing number of students are publishing their work, mostly together with their supervisors, in the standard scientific journals.

Strategies in solving problems or in applying experimental methods require approaches which introduce students to a wide range of problems rather than intensive study of selected topics. Moreover, these problems should not be easy for in this case no genuine problem-solving activity is involved; it is simply a matter of applying a well known routine. In teaching problem solving in pure mathematics at Oxford, about half the students attended problem solving classes where very difficult problems were set, whilst the remaining half continued to attend tutorials (Hammersley, 1968). The performance of students who attended the classes became significantly superior to that of students having tutorials, and at all levels of ability. In applied mathematics classes where problems were relatively easy, no significant advances were achieved relative to the tutorial group. It seems likely that the stimulus of difficulty, together with the variety of attempts and discussion provoked, resulted in acquisition of a greater range of problem solving skills.

In sciences, open-ended experiments are often set in addition, or in preference, to traditional work in which expected results are known in advance. As in projects, this allows for a wide range in performance (Hughes and Morgan, 1970). Even in traditional experimental work it is possible to demand some independent thinking. Read (1969), insists that students should attempt to formulate and to test hypotheses to account for deviations they obtain from expected results.

The effect of continuous assessment of experimental work is said by Chalmers and Stark (1968) to be 'marked improvement and enthusiasm' and greater industry and enjoyment. It is assessed under three headings: accuracy, methodology and comprehension, but since the course is designed to help students in these ways their increased enthusiasm may be due to better understanding rather than to continuous assessment as such. Martin and Lewis (1968) have attempted to clarify the purpose of experimental work for students by designing each experiment to achieve just one objective instead of the usual variety. They claim that this has resulted in considerable improvements in laboratory teaching.

In some cases whole courses have been altered so that experimental work can be relevant and challenging. The Nuffield inter-university biology teaching project (Dowdeswell, 1970) is developing methods which are largely self-instructional – but not costly. These will provide 'bridge courses', 'technique courses' e.g. at Bath, aseptic techniques, and 'main courses' which are short courses that can be inserted anywhere, such as 'Enzymes'. In Electrical Engineering (Jenkins, 1968), in a new university, first years receive sets of questions approximately every six weeks ranging from apparently simple to difficult, and are expected to answer as many as possible using any tools at their disposal. The solution may be theoretical, but if a student decides to carry out an experiment he must first of all design it, then select the equipment, carry out the work and produce the results. The answers to all questions are written in a laboratory log book, which is the only record of the students' work. Even more comprehensive changes have been undertaken at Heriot Watt University (Cowan et al. 1970) where new methods are in use to direct students away from dependence on teachers to a student centred process of genuine education. Learning sessions replace technological lectures and supporting tutorials. Objectives include development of skill in writing and reading, in answering questions and solving problems, making observations and inquiries and in writing reports of observations and deductions. Students make experiments of their own choice and open tutorials are used to deal with unanswered queries.

A survey of first year chemistry courses in Australia (Bryant and Hoare, 1970) shows that practical work in Queensland which 'teaches students to think for themselves' and 'produces data on which to build theory' scores the highest rating for interest.

In biochemistry in one of London's medical schools students circulate to a number of experiments which each provide a surprise, generate a further question or teach a technique which will be required later (Beard and Pole, 1971; Jepson, 1969). Students experiment on themselves or on each other or may have something to show at the end, such as a patient's enzyme pattern. Film loops showing use of experimental techniques are available for students to study when, and as often as, they please. Performance in the laboratory and in group discussion covering experiments made count towards final assessment. Students evidently enjoy this work but no evidence has been collected to show whether they learn more. Organization of a large class to circulate among experiments is discussed here (Jepson, 1969). Other authors who consider this problem, arriving at a number of solutions, are Shouksmith (1969) and Jewell (1970).

Personality and creativity

A new line of inquiry into students' and lecturers' abilities and personalities promises to cast more light on creativity in different fields. Hudson (1966) has distinguished what he terms 'convergent' from 'divergent' thinkers: the former excel in intelligence tests but tend to avoid ambiguity and prefer tests with a single right answer; the latter are comparatively poor in standard tests of intelligence but show great fluency in producing ideas. For example, when asked to think of uses for a brick or a paper clip, the converger mentions one or two uses for each, whereas the diverger produces a large number. 'Divergence' and reasoning, as required in intelligence tests, appear to be fairly unrelated. In addition to individuals biased in either direction, there are 'high all-rounders' who score above the median in both and 'low all-rounders' who score below it in both (Joyce and Hudson, 1968). Those with a bias tend to specialize in different fields – the able convergent thinker chooses physical sciences, the outstanding diverger prefers the arts or administration.

The qualities Hudson finds characteristic of original thinkers of either kind are dedication to work, self-confidence, aggressiveness, a desire to go down in history and a taste for taking risks. Creative workers describe themselves as: inventive, determined, independent, individualistic, enthusiastic and industrious; whereas the non-creative select such adjectives as: responsible, sincere, reliable, dependable, clear thinking, tolerant and understanding.

TEACHING FOR CHANGE OF ATTITUDES

Attitudes and Higher Abilities

In discussion of methods of developing critical thinking we have seen that group discussions exposed prejudices and misconceptions so changing attitudes as well as increasing capacity to think objectively. It is probable that certain attitudes preclude critical thinking or originality, whereas others promote them; the student who clings inflexibly to what he learned at an earlier stage, whether consciously or not, must remain uncritical and any attitude which prevents him from experimenting, such as fear of being proved wrong or looking foolish, is likely to diminish his capacity for finding original solutions or making inventions. To be original it is essential to have an attitude favourable to novelty and exploration. Most probably the development of all higher mental skills is bound up with the concomitant development of favourable attitudes, but there is too little evidence to show this conclusively.

We may reasonably expect increasing attempts to foster understanding of environmental influence on patients and clients in subjects such as medicine, dentistry and law. Some medical schools have already set up departments of social medicine or epidemiology; Davies (1967) suggests that student dentists should 'study the patient and the economic, social and political characteristics of the environment in which he lives' and points out 'that in many ways the success of a dentist depends as much on understanding his patients as persons as upon his technical knowledge and facility'. Students of law also have begun to study sociology.

Such evidence as there is points to group discussion as a more potent method for changing attitudes than lectures or seminars conducted by tutors. A number of research workers have remarked on changes in attitude occurring in group members. Barnett (1958) for example, refers not only to increase in critical thinking but also to an influence on the behaviour of some members in becoming less aggressive. Hallworth (1957) used interpretation of group reactions to make members of a group of teachers more aware of processes influencing them, such as aggressive feelings to authority, and so enabled them to become more self-critical and to develop skills concerned with group management.

For many years group discussion has been a method favoured for training in management. Smith (1969 a, b) outlines the work in group dynamics known as 'T-groups'. As a result of their use, both he (1964, 1969 b) and Cureton (1968) report increases in flexible attitudes and of more considerate behaviour, i.e. of friendliness and sympathy towards others; but groups prove to be differently affected in these respects (Smith and Pollack, 1968). Similar favourable changes in attitudes were noted by Elliott (1958) among engineering employees who took part in T-groups. Changes in actual behaviour were investigated by Moscow (1968) who found greater tolerance, more skill in action and better understanding of others and of group interactions among those who had attended T-groups than their colleagues who had not.

Smith identifies three kinds of social influence operating in groups toward the leader: 'compliance' with some kind of pressure including response to reward, 'identification' with the leader because his personality is attractive, and 'internalization' which occurs when influence is accepted from a leader who is regarded as a trustworthy authority. In a study of 31 groups, Smith (1969 b) found that high identification was not associated with favourable changes in behaviour but resulted in an increase of assertiveness, or dominance, on the part of group members so influenced. Cooper (1968) showed that a substantial positive correlation existed between verified change in subsequent behaviour and group members' perception of the trainer as 'genuine' rather than as masking his true feelings. It is of interest that the factors investigated in considering the leader's effect on the group are relatively unconscious ones. Undoubtedly these are of consequence; but it is commonly believed in universities that students' ability to modify and, more important, to continue to modify their behaviour is more effectively influenced by intellectual factors such as insights into their own assumptions or expectations, through gaining a better under-standing of human relationships or from intellectual acceptance of a value. A tutor's knowledge of group members' management problems seems likely, therefore, to be at least equal in importance with his influence through personal qualities; but this has not been studied.

In discussing acquisition of attitudes we should not forget the simple provision of opportunity to students to actively display affective attributes such as critical judgement and objectivity. Nay and Crocker (1970) have identified a large number of attitudes which science students should be expected to acquire and suggest that they should constitute the basis for curriculum planning.

From reports by individual teachers it is evident that 'games' involving role playing influence attitudes by increasing insight into other people's problems. In one college of art students playing the role of administrative staff developed sympathy towards an unpopular member of staff realizing that he was at the end of a communication line, he received many complaints but had no-one to consult or to pass them to. Similar 'games' have been found helpful with managers in industry, while Ashley (1968) reports role-playing recorded on video tape as an aid to social workers in understanding group interactions and thus to handling human relationships in general.

However, it is possible to use methods which influence attitudes without fostering criticism or insight. In an experiment by King and Irving (1956), students were asked to read a passage, either silently or aloud, advocating extension of the period of military service or, alternatively, to prepare a talk based on the arguments in the passage. Although oral reading gave students the greatest satisfaction, as indicated by their self-ratings, it was the improvized talks which resulted in the speakers accepting the message in the persuasive communication significantly more often than those who merely read it. This seems to be a further example of more efficient 'learning' due to active involvement on the part of the learner. Nevertheless, few teachers would approve this as a method of 'teaching' unless it was used to make students aware that they could be so influenced. The result of this experiment suggests also that choice of textbooks and written exercises, and the unconscious biases of tutors in work they set, may have a more potent influence on students' attitudes than might have been supposed.

An aspect of influence on attitudes that has not been investigated in British universities is imitation of teachers or identification with them by students. There seems to be no doubt that this happens to some extent and it may be partly inability to learn in this way which accounts for antipathy to large classes or complaints by students of lack of contact with staff. Abercrombie (1966) quotes experiments showing the importance of perceived proximity of children to parent figures or teachers and the need for a feeling that authorities are approachable among adults. She comments: 'This feeling of easy access is very important in all sorts of teaching situations, and we can encourage the accessibility or discourage it with minor adjustments of the environment'. However, until investigations are made there are no findings to pass on to teachers who find this difficult to do intuitively.

Motivation

An important objective of teachers is to increase the interest, or motivation, of the majority of students. We have already mentioned some of the factors which contribute to promote them: clear definition of goals with intermediate and immediate objectives, prompt feedback as to success, active, rather than passive, methods of learning and variety in teaching methods. In addition, open-ended problems, dissertations or 'research' projects can arouse considerable enthusiasm.

An experiment which suggests new possibilities of increasing the motivation of students by personality matched courses has been made recently by Joyce and Hudson (1968). It suggests that teachers and students resembling each other with respect to being 'convergent' or 'divergent' types form the most successful combinations in teaching.

Perhaps this has some bearing on a peripheral finding in a study by Lewis and Pask (1964) of communication by mechanical means without verbal interchange. They reported that persons with high IQ were rather bad at communicating, partly because they overrated the receivers' abilities but also because they were more vulnerable to the introduction of misinformation. This looks like the intolerance of convergers to ambiguity. It may be that, in teaching, convergers tend to give a lucid and logically presented account of subject matter, which is acceptable to student convergers, whereas divergent teachers favour digression which sparks off ideas in other divergers but frustrates the convergers' need for good organization. In some cases, however the relationship is more complex and teachers consistently gain a similar degree of success with the same sub-categories of students from one year to another.

EVALUATION OF STUDENTS, TEACHERS AND TEACHING METHODS

Student Selection and Teaching

The usual response of teachers to failure by large numbers of students in examinations is to criticize the examination itself or to demand that selection of students should be improved. It is rare that modification of teaching methods is advocated, or even considered, although evidence exists that these, and the curriculum, may equally be causes of failure. Beard et al. (1964), for example, studied the results of students in two departments of engineering in Birmingham, correlating results in departmental examinations with scores in tests of general reasoning and verbal, numerical and perceptual abilities, as well as inquiring into study habits, social participations of the students and the course content. Correlations between test scores of intellectual abilities and marks in the first-year examinations were preponderantly negative in one department. Consideration of factors likely to result in negative correlations suggested that the most probable cause was insufficient demands on abler students during their first year. Other data from the investigation showed that in this department there was more repetition of school work in the first year, less initial guidance, less pressure to work and less work set, less personal contact between staff and students and more self-education than in the other; there was also a slower pace of work and more students took up distracting activities unrelated to their course of study. Thus, in this instance, the test data indicated ways in which the course could be evaluated and modified.

A different recommendation for improving attainment by students arose from an inquiry to determine predictives of failure by Nisbet and Welsh (1966). Study of first-year performance, in particular, at this Scottish university showed that those in the bottom third of the class in two or more subjects in examinations at the end of the first term were most likely to fail in finals. But it proved that the rate of failure could be reduced by an early warning system following this examination, for feedback as to the probability of failure resulted in greater effort and success. The authors point out that the system is, of course, more effective when work in the first term is similar to that in the second and third years.

More recently Halpin (1968) has come to a similar conclusion that all students who had two subject failures in the second veterinary examination should be given careful counselling since there was a rather greater possibility that they would fail in the final examinations.

When subjects differ essentially in content in different years of the course prediction of success from year to year is much less certain. Furneaux correlated examinations results for students at the end of their first and second years of a course (Furneaux, 1962). On the whole correlations were poor and attainments in first-year Applied Electricity, for example, correlated more highly with second year mathematics (0.69) than did first-year mathematics (0.47). Thus the practice of insisting that a student should pass in first-year work before proceeding to the second in this subject seemed unjustified. In addition, students' examination results were influenced by personality characteristics, introverts with neurotic tendencies doing significantly better than stable extroverts. But this, too, may be due to curricula and to methods of teaching and learning normally employed in the university. Furneaux comments '.... it became clear that the problem which confronts us is really that of understanding the way in which the characteristics of the student and of the university interact to determine particular outcomes.'

That A-level results are a poor indication of success in degree courses in sciences is shown by the findings of Bagg (1968). Richards and Wilson (1961) and Elton (1968). Bagg found that for a small sample three A-level science results correlated negatively with marks in a technology; while, for chemical engineers, the summed total of A-level results was a somewhat better predictor than the result in chemistry or any other subject. Richards and Wilson reported that the failure rate of students entering physics courses with the highest A-level results was as great as 15 per cent, and, in a survey of physics departments, Elton finds little predictive value in A-level results except that those with high grades are more likely to get some kind of degree than those with low grades. However, of nine students entering with E grades, five received honours degrees. Elton's main finding is that in university departments with identical entrance standards, 42, 38 and 72 per cent of students gained honours degrees. He concludes that 'the attainment of a student at a university may depend almost as much on the idiosyncrasy of the university as on the ability of the student', and points to evidence of different standards in teaching in departments of London University which take the same examinations.

Evidently, in addition to those factors normally considered in selection problems – such as students' abilities and interests, their previous experience and the nature of the entrance examination – reduction in failures can also result from changes in teaching, modifications in the course, improved staff-student relations or more information to the student as to the success of his learning.

Methods of Assessment and Teaching

Since one of the chief objectives of students in entering university is to obtain a qualification, the form of assessment employed has a considerable influence on emphases in content and methods of study. The effectiveness of teaching and of teaching methods is therefore influenced by the ways in which students are assessed.

In the past the only universal evaluation technique was the terminal, or final, examination which was used to rank students and to determine whether they had attained an 'agreed standard'. Numerous inquiries during the last thirty years or so have shown how ineffectively traditional exams, employing essay questions, oral and practical tests, achieved these objectives (Beard, 1970; Cox, 1967). There is a demand today for more varied types of assessment to meet the variety of aims in teaching as well as for more evaluation of learning and teaching during courses. Black reports of an inquiry into university examinations in physics (1968): 'In general, departments replied that they had not formulated rules about the style of questions, did not analyze systematically the abilities tested by the questions, did not ask for model answers and did not ask for a marking scheme'. There were no multiple choice examinations, the questions being of the bookwork-essay type or in two parts — bookwork followed by a problem. All the questions were of the same style, different papers testing different topics but not different types of ability.

Similar limitations have been found in studies of chemistry examinations and of examinations in biochemistry (Beard and Pole, 1971). But, in the latter case, some papers allow, or require, a wider range of cognitive skills. In one medical school a new type of examination for the second MB has been devised in four parts: a multiple choice paper to test factual knowledge or simple problems, a long essay for which six weeks preparation is allowed so that students are encouraged to seek information for themselves and to think originally, a paper of five traditional essay questions and a paper requiring students to evaluate experimental data in response to the question: 'explain as fully as you can what you consider is happening and try to account for all the results recorded. Give some brief theoretical background against which the problem and your solution can be set. Indicate what further investigation would help test correctness of your explanation'.

Despite the findings of these investigations, a substantial number of teachers are relatively uncritical of traditional types of examinations. In a study among micro-biologists in the United Kingdom and Ireland, essay-type questions and orals were found to be almost universal and practical examinations were used by just over half. It was generally felt that term-time assessment of practicals would be more satisfactory, but teachers wished to keep the existing form of examination in theory (Stewart-Tull, 1970).

A different pattern of examining in physics is reported by Elton (1968). At Surrey the final assessment is based on (1) examinations at the end of the sixth and the beginning of the ninth terms, which each carry about a third of the marks and (2) course work assessments, under five headings: (a) an essay written in the first summer vacation; (b) an open-book oral examination at the end of the fifth term; (c) full reports on three experiments selected by the examiners from those in the laboratory during the second year; (d) an oral examination on two other experiments, 30 minutes notice being given as to which ones, and (e) a project which is undertaken during the whole of the final term. Account is also taken of the level of the courses chosen during the first two years. Elton comments that although the reliability of marks for course work is low, the validity is high.

A development towards greater diversity in examining in the arts is described by Brockbank (1969). Staff of the English department at York have retained the three hour paper to test alacrity, rapid command of material and good recall, but they have introduced a variety of other forms of assessment. These include a 14 day paper limited to 1200 words, to encourage refinement of thinking and expression and a keen sense of relevance. Five tutorial essays are also submitted at the end of term for formal assessment, following rewriting after discussion with the tutor. Students may choose to be assessed in oral work in delivering, defending and discussing a paper. In addition, long essays of seven to ten thousand words are assessed, some subsequent to tutorial guidance and others without, and an ancillary viva may be used in conjunction with any written form of assessment. It is of interest that about two-thirds of the students achieve comparable grades by any method, one sixth each do better in papers written at leisure or in traditional papers, while one-tenth of these do either better or worse than by continuous assessment.

In medicine multiple choice tests are in fairly common use in terminal assessments and in some final examinations (Beard, 1967 b). Anderson (1967) advocates in-course testing to motivate students to achieve their maximum performance. He points out the need to devise tests of clinical skills and habits that the student has acquired in relation to history taking, clinical examination of the patient, bedside tests, etc. and suggests the use of microphones to aid assessment of the students' abilities in taking histories. The Todd Report also recommends the use of continuous assessment in clinical courses (Royal Commission on Medical Education, 1968).

The influence of methods of assessment upon the effectiveness of teaching and teaching methods varies also with students' attitudes, personality traits and aims. Walton and Drewery (1967) found that of those who did badly in an objective test in psychiatry the majority were highly extraverted; they were not good at medical examinations in general, not so good clinically, were prone to express value judgements to patients and to give advice, and were inclined at the beginning of the course to consider psychiatry irrelevant to their future professional work. Low scorers expressed disappointment with the amount and quality of teaching about drugs and physical treatments whereas high scorers wished for more teaching in psychology and sociology.

Malleson (1967) also found that, in the case of clinical students, high drive introverts did best and low drive extroverts were the least successful, whereas in the second MB there was no difference between these groups. He suggested that the second MB course was so highly structured and controlled that there was little latitude for the individual's personality to influence his attainment.

Other researchers have also shown the superiority of introverts as examinees. Davis and Mowbray (1968) found that students with high introversion scores had a very significantly higher mark in psychiatry. The Entwistles (1970) who explored the relationship between personality, study methods and academic performance, report that introverted first year students had a better academic record, slightly better study methods (i.e. they worked more carefully) thought ahead, were conscientious and recognized the importance of working conditions. In a second study, with Wilson (1970), performance proved to be strongly related with study methods, motivation and introversion scores but had no relation with emotional stability. A study-methods scale distinguished between the worst students and the best, and the extraversion score between the best and the remainder. They recommend questionnaires on motivation and study methods as a means of detecting potential failures for remedial action. Differences between introverts and extraverts have prompted other inquiries. Leith and Wisdom (1970) found that introverts did better with more structured methods whereas extraverts fared better with less structured ones. Trown (1970) showed in a number of studies that among children introverts were superior in performance when rules were presented before examples, whereas extraverts were superior when examples were presented first. This held good for immediate learning, retention and transfer of learning to similar situations. In addition, it held good for different levels of both intelligence and anxiety. Thus the common finding that introverts do better in university courses may be as much a reflection on the courses and examinations as on the students.

Assessment of course work has not yet been studied in any detail. Commonly used methods such as exercises, essays, problems, etc. which are marked some time after the student completes the work are being increasingly criticized because they often fail to detect causes of students' difficulties, tend to be marked uninformatively and provide corrections, if any, too late to influence learning at the critical time. Three new types of evaluation are being developed to give more objective and immediate assessment both to teacher and student.

Evaluation of Teachers

The first attempt to evaluate university teaching concentrated on qualities of the teacher. Possibly this was inspired by a desire to reward the best teachers in university departments even if they were not outstanding research workers for it is generally believed that it is excellence in research alone which gains advancement. Rating scales were devised in America and were later modified for use abroad. In Queensland, for example, students were invited to express their reactions to their teachers' performances with a view to obtaining a group opinion from a set list of characteristics of teachers (Schonell et al., 1961). A teacher meeting with the students' approval might find that, in his case, students had underlined such statements as: 'knows subject thoroughly; interested in teaching; never stops learning; always well prepared; presents material in systematic fashion; uses varied methods; sets high standards; ....; has a sense of humour'. Whereas for his less fortunate colleague they might endorse: 'Often does not know subject; is unsystematic, vague and rambling; has no clear standards; shows undesirable personal qualities such as laziness, impatience, prejudice, intolerance; has annoying mannerisms; will not admit errors; ....' But attempts to achieve group views in this way, which really had a bearing on teaching, were unsuccessful. Teachers perform differently when they teach different topics, or classes of different abilities, or when they employ different teaching methods; they may even perform well in one university department and indifferently in another. Students, or colleagues, also differ in the way they assess teaching; some praise highly a conscientious teacher who covers the syllabus thoroughly in well organized lectures while others look for inspiration and originality, preferring to obtain basic information in private study.

Ratings of one particular teacher on 44 characteristics, on two occasions separated by two and a half years, correlated significantly (0.71) (Foy, 1969). But although this suggests that students' assessments are fairly reliable, it cannot confirm their validity. Indeed, Leyton (1966) suggests that students build stereotypes of their lecturers.

Assessment of Teaching

In more recent studies of teaching, therefore, it is the teaching itself which is assessed, either by testing how much information students have gained or by inquiring early in a course whether the teaching could be adjusted in any way to meet students' needs more fully. In some departments frequent testing is used for the information of staff and students. In the department of Mechanical Engineering, University of Birmingham, weekly quizzes (brief written tests) are used in this way, a generally poor result being accepted as a reflection on teaching in that topic (Beard et al., 1964).

Inquiries into the effectiveness of a teacher's communication with his class cover a wider range of information: students may be asked to endorse one of five statements about the amount of material during a period of teaching: 'far too much, ..., satisfactory, ... practically nothing worth saying,' or of speed 'spoken too fast, ..., about right, ... tediously slow,' etc., as well as making comments on conditions in the room, use of audio-visual aids, value and quality of applications or examples, adequacy of answers to questions, and so on (Beard, 1967 b; McVey, 1967). In this way, even if the replies are somewhat damaging to the teacher's self-esteem, he has a guide to future action which should enable him to communicate better with that group of students.

For evaluation of teaching, Wragg (1970) used the Flanders' Interaction Technique. This involves allocating the teacher's and pupils' contributions to one of 10 categories at regular short intervals, say every three seconds: e.g. praises or encourages, asks question, lectures or gives facts etc., students initiate talk, silence and confusion. To his surprise he found 'an almost unbelievably stable pattern'. Analysis of the first 35,000 tallies collected by students of education showed more than a third of the time given to 'lecturing', nearly a quarter to 'silence and confusion' and about an eighth each to teachers asking questions or to pupils' responses. Bligh (1971) describes a modification of this technique suitable for use in small group teaching in higher education. Where the teacher plays a minor role (at least overtly) or where the emotive aspects of students' contributions are important – as in tutorials or 'free group discussion' – he recommends the use of Bales' Interaction Process Analysis which is described by Sprott (1958) in Human Groups (p. 130-132).

As a more direct measure of the achievement of teaching objectives, Bligh (b) has developed a 'Truth Functional Test' at eight cognitive levels. The test consists of statements to which students may respond 'agree', 'disagree' or 'don't know' and which bear a precise and specifiable logical relation to statements used in teaching. This is quick to administer and to mark, it is easier to construct than multiple choice questions and encourages less guessing, and it may be modified for affective objectives or an infinite number of cognitive levels. It has in addition the unique feature of being objective both in setting and marking, and is suitable for use during a period of teaching to obtain prompt feedback.

Evaluation of on-going learning

The previously mentioned findings of psychologists' that correct responses in learning should be speedily reinforced, or wrong ones as speedily corrected, do not meet with ready acceptance among all university teachers. There seems to be a prevalent feeling that students are mature enough to wait for their corrections; but, although they may be expected to wait with patience, the evidence is that, in any learning, prompt feedback leads to greater efficiency. This is, of course, one of the advantages of programmed learning.

Various methods have been devised, or arrived at intuitively, which do provide feedback to every student on his recall and understanding of informational material, or test his grasp of principles and how to apply them, and all have been found extremely effective (Beard, 1967 b). Such methods normally include (i) questions for students to answer (e.g. short answer items, multiple-choice questions, short problems or brief essay questions), (ii) immediate provision of correct answers or discussion by students of their answers and opportunity to look up further information, putting any outstanding questions to the tutor, (iii) correction of the students' records for use in revision. The tutor may also set practical work depending on the information gained, or recommend further related study. These methods have the double merit that the students can assess their own learning and retain corrected records, while the tutor obtains feedback on the effectiveness of his teaching from the students' failures, questions, or enthusiasm for further inquiry.

Students' opinions of teaching methods

Students' opinions of teaching methods have been inquired into on a number of occasions. The Hale and Robbins Reports (University Grants Committee, 1964; Committee on Higher Education, 1963) survey opinions of students in the majority of universities and colleges. Marris (1965) obtained views from students of three universities and one technical college. The NUS Report of 1969 (Saunders, 1969) gives views of students of two universities, two technical colleges, two art colleges and two colleges of education. Views of medical students were collected and published in 1965 and, a year later, students of the Royal Dental College published a report of their views on lecturing in the college. McLeish (1970) and Stones (1969) have inquired into the opinions of students in colleges of education. In addition, surveys of students' views have been made in Australia (Australian Vice-Chancellors' Committee, 1963; Schonell et al., 1962), by individuals in single colleges and by research workers in the course of investigations into teaching methods.

In general there is considerable criticism of lectures. The Hale Report concludes: 'The general tenor of the student memoranda is very similar. It is highly critical of the lecture. The principal desiderata are fewer and better lectures, closer staff-student relations, and more teaching by tutorial and seminar.' In reply to the invitation to distinguish characteristics of good and bad lectures, 44 per cent mentioned points of delivery such as audibility, speed of delivery, diction and legibility of writing on the board, 43 per cent commented on clarity and order, 36 per cent stressed the importance of interest; scientists, in particular, remarked on their need for ease in taking notes, non-scientists referred fairly frequently to the desirability of originality and about 20 per cent of all students emphasized that lectures should be comprehensible and should provide a guide to further study. Overall percentages obtained in Marris' inquiry were fairly similar, but, in addition, about 20 per cent of students felt a need for more guidance.

Despite their stringent criticisms of lecturing, when asked what changes they would propose only $12\frac{1}{2}$ per cent in Oxbridge and 20 per cent in London (with intermediate proportions in other universities) suggested fewer lectures. One may conclude, perhaps, that it is lecturing technique rather than the method itself which is criticized. In the unofficial surveys made for the report, 65 per cent of all students who replied wished for no change in the proportion of lectures, 14 per cent expressed a wish for fewer lectures, but 10 per cent would have welcomed more. On the other hand, when asked similar questions about tutorials and seminars, the vast majority of those already having some wished for more; in Sheffield, for example, 73 per cent wanted more while merely four per cent wished for fewer; only in Cambridge where tutorials are more frequent was there substantially less desire for an increase in their number.

The NUS report of 1969 (Saunders et al., 1969) gives average hours per week spent in formal lectures in the pairs of colleges investigated as: four (art college), 14 (education), $12\frac{1}{2}$ (technical) and eight (universities), but the students from art colleges spent 30 hours per week in studio work. Preferences they stated suggest that the university students were content, but that those having more lectures would have liked fewer: education, 12, technical 10, but art students would have welcomed five hours in place of four. In these eight colleges, three hours per week was typical of the time spent in seminars, except in the college of art (one hour), and less than two hours were spent in tutorials except in the technical college (three hours). Student teachers wished for six hours in seminars, but other students would have preferred about three hours each in seminars and tutorials. The average time students wished to spend in practicals and written work corresponded closely with the time they did spend.

When asked to rate teaching methods for effectiveness, 58 per cent of the students rated lectures as effective, but other types of teaching were more likely to be rated 'very effective', indicating a preference for smaller groups and personal teaching.

The Report on Medical Education by the British Medical Students' Association is a source of student opinion on teaching methods which is representative of a large sample, although possibly not a statistically representative one. Students considered that, in general, they were given insufficient opportunity to play an active part in their own education, they advocated a reduction in the number of lectures, but improvement in the standard of remaining ones, partly by increased use of such audio-visual aids as films, slides, charts and demonstrations. Methods advocated to increase students' participation were the Grand Tutorial and Corlab in both of which students arrive already prepared for questioning or discussion. There was also considerable demand for more tutorials to cope with individual difficulties and a request for more extensive use of the new media. These views are to some extent supported by recommendations in the Todd Report (1965-6) which advocates a considerable reduction in the number of lectures.

In 1969, Hawkins reviewed students' opinions on practical biochemistry in the London medical colleges (Hawkins, 1969). Two thirds of the students enjoyed it 'a little' or 'not at all' and one half felt that it was no help in understanding the subject. Just under half felt that substitution of demonstrations of modern apparatus and techniques for practical work would make the courses fully comprehensible, and more than four fifths favoured additional tutorials. A majority preferred experimental work (if it continued) to consist of short experiments with an occasional long project.

A point on which opinions differed between Australian students and their teachers, and which is frequently raised in Britain also, is the provision of duplicated notes. 83 per cent of Australian students liked them because they found them closer to the course, more accurate than their own notes and useful in revision (Australian Vice-Chancellor's Committee, 1963). In Britain students more often mention the waste of time and hindrance to understanding which result from taking notes (Marris, 1965; Saunders, 1969). Australian teachers were divided, some regarding notes as spoon feeding, an encouragement to 'swotting' from notes only and to passivity on the part of students; these pointed to the strain on secretarial resources and the consequent tendency to use the same notes from year to year. But no-one, it seems, objected to laboratory notes, field notes or instructions for experimental work or to bibliographies and essay or reading lists. Those who favoured use of duplicated notes considered that they saved time for the lecturer, allowed him to digress profitably without leading his students to lose sight of the central argument, compensated for lack of suitable books or for library deficiencies and might incorporate journal material that was not readily accessible. The inquiry showed that the kind of notes provided differed widely — from brief outlines provided in advance, or occasional summaries, to verbatim reports of most lectures or very full notes comprising hundreds of pages which served as the department's 'text-book'. It is the latter which is most generally disapproved by students. As we have already seen in an earlier section (Elton et al., 1970; MacManaway, 1970) there is now some evidence that duplicated notes can be highly effective when well designed and used to promote activity on the part of students. Students consulted for the NUS report regarded seminars as important for interchange of ideas, stimulus of creative thinking and improvement of self-expression but less suitable for consolidation of learning and study in depth. Common complaints were of

'domination by one or two students', dependence on staff, bad and insufficient preparatory work by students. Most thought that ideally there should not be more than ten people participating and that the seminars should not last for more than one hour. In a survey of more than one thousand college of education students by Stones (1969) over half preferred seminars to lectures and tutorials; they were rated highest for developing standards of judgement, inspiring ideas, learning to present an argument, discussion of practical work and revision. They considered tutorials most useful for obtaining feed-back on progress, feeling known and planning future work. In the NUS report over half the students thought the major functions of tutorials were to consult tutors on work or other matters and to receive detailed criticism of prepared work, but opinion was evenly divided whether an academic tutor should be the same person who advised on personal problems. Over half thought that tutorial groups should meet once a week and should contain a maximum of three students.

However, not all students think alike. In one College of Education, Woolford (1969) found that although on the whole students preferred methods encouraging participation, more intelligent and less stable students preferred restricted participation whilst introverted students only slightly preferred these methods to more formal ones. In an investigation relating personality traits with attitudes to lectures, seminars and tutorials, McLeish (1968) found eight roughly distinguishable types. These ranged from 'enthusiasts' who liked all methods to rebels who liked none. Others markedly favoured methods in which lectures played a major part or those which emphasized student participation. The former of these two groups appeared to be tough minded introverts with high security need, tending to be submissive and to favour formal methods and having high scholastic values. The latter valued new experience and freedom for themselves more strongly than other groups and were more anxious; they were also more radical in their educational views and more extraverted. In a later study (1970) in colleges of education he found lectures to be unpopular with independently minded students and with those who believed that the educational system required substantial change; they were favoured by older, more conservative, stable, submissive, unsure or religious students. Those favouring lectures took a more favourable view of the staff, and the converse was also true.

Students within one school or one discipline serve to show the diversity of responses. Joyce and Weatherall (1959) found that a sample of their students enjoyed discussions initiated by tape recording more than seminars conducted by teachers; they returned singly, or in small groups, to listen again to the recordings more often than students attending seminars returned for further information or discussion. However, they considered seminars more useful than discussions. Lectures were considered by all groups to be outstandingly the most useful methods, and three quarters of the students considered them most enjoyable. Reading was considered almost as useful as practicals but much less enjoyable. In this study the authors point out that an overall slight negative correlation between total estimates of usefulness and enjoyment with final marks in three sections of the text suggest that the more critical students performed better and the less critical less well. In an earlier study (1957) there was negligible correlation between students' impressions of their enjoyment of a method and success in corresponding tests. They observed 'It follows that performance and students' judgements cannot both be criteria of the efficiency of teaching methods'. On the other hand, since different teaching methods tend to foster different intellectual skills, the method of testing could favour one unduly.

In an Australian study (Kitchen, 1969) external students experiencing a wide range of teaching methods including tape-recordings, tutors' visits, correspondence, written assignments, lectures and 'vacation schools' rated the methods on a variety of criteria. Students were generally satisfied with teaching but a well planned library proved to be most highly valued. Students differed most in valuing different major means of study, in preferring teaching methods with informal and more personal kinds of teaching and in concern for spoken and oral aspects.

Familiarity with high standards of professional television might lead students to be critical of the efforts of their teacher, but the reaction of radiologists at Glasgow (Davidson and Thompson, 1970) was overwhelmingly favourable. However, James (1970) found that although students preferred learning from videotape, they were more successful when using an instruction booklet. Students of psychiatry considered CCTV to be more effective than either programmed instruction or the conventional case demonstration; and as measured by a multiple choice test, the second judgement was correct, but the first was incorrect.

Neale (1967) used live demonstrations, relayed television, recorded television and a lecture, to lead classroom technique and found that students preference was in the order which reflected immediacy, or reality of the experience.

It is of interest that there is so much to report about students' and teachers' opinions of different teaching methods but that there are still relatively few inquiries into their effects on learning. Although consumer satisfaction deserves some consideration, in the long run it is measures of effective learning which count towards students' success and contribute most to improvements in teaching method.

Assessment of Courses

We observed earlier that no studies of courses in British universities had so far been published. However, studies of entire courses are now in progress in seven universities in England and, although they are necessarily longitudinal, some results may soon be available. Otherwise, attempts to evaluate courses are limited to inquiries into 'consumer satisfaction'. In this respect, medical schools in London have made considerable progress for the majority of teachers replying to a questionnaire reported that they 'always' (25 per cent) 'frequently' (25 per cent) or 'sometimes' (27 per cent) invited criticisms or suggestions from their students about courses or teaching (Beard, 1967 b). Teachers in three of the dental schools probably corresponded more nearly with the majority of university teachers, the corresponding percentages being approximately: 20, 16 and 28.

Reid-Smith attempted to measure student satisfaction with a course in librarianship taught chiefly by lectures, seminars and syndicate method. Opposing opinions were recorded but mature students were uniformly more appreciative. It was clear that students had not thought about the purpose of this course except to get a qualification. Except for sessions spent in reporting back, syndicates were the most popular. Discussion in the local bar was more popular than those elsewhere.

In a post-graduate school where every item of a teaching programme was graded on a three point scale, a fall was reported in the number of dissatisfied course members, staff were stimulated by knowing that they were assessed and students co-operated more willingly (Gauvain, 1968). In the later report Gauvain (1970) concludes that the aims of a course should be made known to students. Students should be asked to state their aims in applying to attend, and course assessments by students should always be followed by discussion.

The difficulty of satisfying all the students in a course of lectures is stressed by Falk (1967) who recorded comments by four students on the same series of lectures in history :-

(1)   Made a fascinating period of history very flat.

(2)   Congratulations on an exceedingly workmanlike job of teaching as opposed to purely lecturing.

(3)   Gives students impression that they are back in the schoolroom. By this I mean over-simplification, over-clarification.

(4)   These lectures were the best I've had this year.

It is true that the range of ability among first year students in Australia is very wide, but even in England the opinions of teaching capacity of lecturers tends to vary from student to student and as classes change from year to year.

COURSES AND SERVICES FOR UNIVERSITY TEACHERS

During the last few years, and in particular since 1970, British universities and colleges have begun to organize short courses for new teachers and some-times for experienced ones also. Rayner (1966) describes courses in Australia of a kind now fairly familiar in Britain, in which staff hear lectures on univer-sity policy, teaching methods etc., attend classes on voice production and public speaking, and discuss the aims of university teaching, methods of examin-ing and assessment of students' work, the functions of different teaching methods and university discipline. Such courses normally occupy several consecutive days or evenings of one term, or even a day per week for a whole year. In Queensland the sessions valued most are those on university facilities such as closed-circuit television and teaching aids, practice sessions on seminar leader-ship and discussion of examination techniques. In London, where rather similar courses are run for new lecturers, sessions most appreciated are those in which the participants are themselves active (Reports and Proceedings, 1968); there has been a demand particularly from younger lecturers, to keep lectures short and to maximize time for discussion.

Television is used increasingly to show teachers their own performances and to allow them to see and to discuss the teaching of their colleagues. Where a television centre exists teachers are assisted in planning programmes of their own. In every case there are opportunities to analyze teaching skills and methods of presentation.

McKevvitt (1967) reports an experiment at Stanford University in which teachers are recorded on videotape and view their performances later, either in company or alone. They are instructed to look for such points as (1) skill in pre-instructional procedures e.g. establishment of rapport, provoking interest and giving cues as to what will follow .... (4) skill in pacing e.g. pauses and moments of silence, time to ask questions, to facilitate transition from one point to another and in introduction of a new idea, etc. This method stimulates self-improvement, facilitates guidance and makes possible a study of variables involved in teaching.

Provision of services to teachers takes a variety of forms. At Melbourne, courses for teachers and studies of teaching are provided jointly by the University Teaching Project Office and the Education Research Office (Falk, 1966). The former has developed a variety of services to Faculties, Departments and individual members of staff; these comprise (1) empirical studies of existing teaching and learning practices which are undertaken at the request of the departments concerned; (2) considerations with the staff, of the theory by which such practices can be evaluated; (3) courses of training, largely based on the findings of (1) and (2); (4) a consultant service for members of staff whose needs are not met by the courses. This service includes visits to classes, discussions and help as required e.g. with speech therapy, construction of course notes and other techniques of teaching; (5) co-operation with Departments in the planning of new courses and in the use of new aids and techniques; (6) basic research, when pressure for services permits this. Investigations under heading (1) normally involve a full report from staff and students as to the efficacy of teaching methods, techniques of evaluation, etc. but the findings are confidential until such time as a large body of comparative data is available.

In London working methods are fairly similar, but the University Teaching Methods Unit is part of the Institute of Education and therefore has many educational experts to draw on as tutors or speakers at courses, in addition to the many specialist teachers of London University who assist in these ways. London University also offers exceptional opportunities because it has many constituent colleges; it is therefore possible to bring together groups of people who share the same problems. The Unit has initiated a number of co-operative projects and has been able to set up a Medical Research Section whose members suggest and share in inquiries and researches. Since the University decided to increase the size of the Unit in 1970, working parties have been set up to extend research already in progress by specifying objectives in a number of subjects and relating these with methods in teaching and evaluation. Several of the staff are interested also in problems of evaluation.

Other universities having departments with a special concern with teaching in higher education are Aston and Lancaster. Both run induction courses for new lecturers and seminars for other teaching staff, in addition to conducting research into teaching and learning.

A different arrangement exists in Sheffield where a panel of 12 senior teaching staff act as counsellors to newly appointed members. If invited to do so, they give advice on planning lectures and use of equipment or criticize performance in lecturing.

Some audio-visual departments have also developed a particular concern with improvement of teaching methods. At Heriot-Watt University methods are studied in the process of planning and improving sessions of television teaching. At Stirling, a substantial grant has been obtained for trial of micro-teaching as an aid to student teachers.

Other centres were developed specifically to improve teaching in sciences as at Surrey and Chelsea (in London), or in one science, i.e. chemistry, at East Anglia. The last of these, together with enthusiastic teachers of chemistry throughout the country, has given impetus to the professional bodies of chemists to investigate examining, and to set up working parties to study uses of audio-visual aids and the development of programmed texts.

Since 1969-70, a large number of British universities have formed working parties of academic staff, including representatives of research groups or education departments, to take responsibility for organizing courses for new lecturers and for the improvement of teaching. They initiate inquiries into teaching and arrange demonstrations of teaching methods.

The method favoured in medical schools in the United States and Canada is to provide a complete educational unit to serve each one. The function of its staff is to aid the teachers in specifying their objectives, in designing the courses and in selection of methods in teaching and assessment. In addition, the psychologists (or educational experts) evaluate teaching and learning and develop methods of improving them. In this way teachers and students receive constant feedback on their performance and the course is continuously monitored and improved. Since the ratio of psychologists to teaching staff may be as high as one to 10, this is a luxury service which cannot usually be offered in Britain. However, there is a parallel in the Open University which has appointed an educational technologist to each course team to ensure that educational principles are applied in the process of course design; the educator works on equal terms with the subject experts and the BBC representative. In addition, a few university departments have Research Units set up to provide a service of this kind. At the Bartlett School of Architecture in London, Dr Abercrombie and her colleagues are attempting to raise the general level of awareness of educational problems and to improve competence in teaching, mainly through discussion. While funds permitted, Flood Page worked with dental staff of the London Hospital Medical School with a view to improving teaching there.

A fuller account of courses and services in each university in Britain has been published by the Society for Research into Higher Education (Greenaway, 1971).

In view of criticisms at the level of secondary education where research into teaching methods and the training of teachers are conducted largely independently of teachers in the schools, the determination of university teachers to play an active role in investigating teaching methods seems highly desirable. For otherwise there is a danger that new ideas will be developed in the colleges of education, or in psychology departments but will not be adequately communicated or accepted by the teachers. For example, an inquiry by Maddox (1968) showed that one teacher training course suffered a number of deficiencies: 'few students had an opportunity to observe a range of teachers, many had no close or detailed supervision, the general academic instruction which preceded the practice period in teaching, even if cognitively accepted, seldom influenced classroom practice. Innovations, therefore, tended not to be effectively communicated to student teachers, many of whom continued to use methods they were familiar with as pupils'. Raitt (1968) who studied teacher training of graduate chemists found that most departments of education had inadequate laboratory facilities and that five-sixths of the departments gave less than the 63 hours teaching in chemistry which was the estimated bare minimum to meet the needs which teachers in training expressed. He lists the chief requirements in training which were mentioned by young teachers and adds that, on the whole, the teachers felt that they had not been adequately helped in these respects. This kind of situation would be unlikely to arise if there was close co-operation between teachers and each department of education or if some teachers served as part-time tutors in the departments.

Several recent investigations in colleges and departments of education are more encouraging and have relevance for teachers throughout higher education. Ishler (1967) reports an experiment in which use of feedback to student teachers was effective in making their behaviour more student-centred. McFarlane Smith has shown (but has not yet published) that the course at Garnett College is effective in developing attitudes favourable to rapport and harmonious relations. A study by Crocker (1968) of characteristics of students, rated as good or poor teachers, indicated that the poor teachers scored low in flexibility in verbal thinking. In a different study (Davies, 1968) poor student teachers proved to be less anxious than those rated as average or able, having personality profiles similar to those of clerks or secretaries. Bishop and Levy (1968) made an inquiry into dimensions of behaviour which tutors considered in assessing teaching. As a result, they suggest that certain basic skills, which are not subject specific, could be practised collectively by student teachers before concentrating on more complex matters of method and approach for their individual subjects.

Of more specific interest to tutors in Colleges of Education is an inquiry of Cope (1969) into students attitudes and problems in relation to teaching practice.

If training is to be introduced for university teachers there are several obvious recommendations; firstly, objectives in teacher training should be very fully considered; secondly, university teachers (especially those beginning to teach) should be consulted as to their needs, and reports by students on teaching methods should be studied; thirdly, university teachers should share in the responsibility for any courses that are planned and should play an active part in them; fourthly, they should increasingly introduce innovations or undertake experiments in teaching methods, possibly being allowed free time to do so. In this way, the role of psychologists and specialists in education will be that of consultants only and a high level of interest in teaching methods is likely to be maintained, or developed in university departments.

CONCLUSIONS

Inquiry or research into teaching and learning in higher education is gaining momentum. Of the references cited here seven date from before 1950, 20 were published between 1950 and 1959, over 280 between 1960 and 1969, and there are already 55 in 1970 alone; hundreds more investigations or experiments are in preparation. Interest in teaching methods at this level has grown considerably, most notably in medical schools, but courses and conferences on teaching are well attended and new journals devoted to education in biology, engineering, chemistry, physics, medicine and mathematics point to a new, or increasing, concern with the effectiveness of teaching and learning. Many more teachers are now initiating inquiries or experiments. From the foregoing survey, it is evident that there is much for them to do. Only very limited conclusions can be drawn from the studies so far completed, yet changing subject matter and curricula, increasing numbers of students and the introduction of further new techniques in teaching continue to give rise to fresh problems.

In areas where experiments or inquiries have been most numerous, developments are likely to follow fairly rapidly. Increased efficiency in teaching may be expected in the near future, partly through linking schools and departments by closed-circuit television so that lectures and demonstrations can reach a wider audience, and partly by the use of other new techniques in class teaching or for individual study, such as programmed learning, audio- or video-tape and slides or film-loops with tapes.

However, where experimental work has been less adequate, carefully planned sequences of experiments or inquiries are still needed. It is not usually possible to draw general conclusions from comparison of one teaching method with another on one occasion in a single department. What is needed is a concerted effort in studying each method, collating information already available, and experimenting with variations of the method to see which ones are most effective and under what circumstances. Since, for various reasons, small group discussions are used increasingly this is one area in which well-designed experiments in a cross section of schools would be particularly rewarding. Other investigations which are likely to prove most rewarding are those into higher mental abilities and students' methods of studying. Such knowledge will enable teachers to gain more insight into students' difficulties and to devise more flexible methods of teaching which take account of their differences.

Increasing acceptance of the desirability of evaluating courses, teaching and learning should lead to a more precise formulation of objectives, for realistic evaluation is impossible unless objectives are clearly defined. Perhaps also some teachers and students need to change their attitudes to routine evaluation, accepting it as necessary feed-back to ensure the efficient operation of the learning process rather than as damaging criticism of personal competence.

Research into teaching methods in higher education is now expanding rapidly. It remains for teachers and psychologists to ensure that the most pressing and fundamental problems are investigated and on a sufficiently large scale to have general application. In this way we may hope to build up a theory of teaching and learning which will enable us to solve new problems as they arise and to design courses which will achieve our objectives with certainty.

REFERENCES

ABERCROMBIE, M.L.J. (1965) The Anatomy of Judgment, London, Huchinson

ABERCROMBIE, M.L.J. (1966) Perception and communication in Teaching Methods in University Departments of Science and Medicine, report of a conference held at the University of London Institute of Education, January 1966 (out of print)

ABERCROMBIE, M.L.J. (1970) Aims and Techniques of Group Teaching, London, Society for Research into Higher Education

ABERCROMBIE, M.L.J. (1968) The work of a university education research unit. Universities Quarterly, 22 (2), 182-196

ADAM, J.B. and SHAWCROSS, A.J. (1963) Language Laboratory, London, Pitmans

ADAMS, B.G., DANIEL, E.E., HERXHEIMER, A. and WEATHERALL, M. (1960) The value of emphasis in eliminating errors. British Medical Journal, 1960 (2), 1007-1011

ADAMSON, H. and MERCER, F.V. (1970) A new approach to undergraduate biology II kits and the open laboratory for internal students. Journal of Biological Education, 4, 167-176

ALDERMAN, G.H. (1926) Improving comprehension ability in silent reading. Journal of Educational Research, 13 (1), 11-21

ALLEN, H.G. (1968) Engineering projects for engineering undergraduates in Innovations and Experiments in University Teaching Methods, 81-87. University Teaching Methods Research Unit, London, University of London Institute of Education

AMARIA, R.P., BIRAN, L.A. and LEITH, G.O.M. (1969) Individual versus co-operative learning I: influence of intelligence and sex. Educational Research, 11 (2), 95-103

AMARIA, R.P. and LEITH, G.O.M. (1969) Individual versus co-operative learning II : the influence of personality. Educational Research, 11 (3), 193-199

AMSWYCH, R.J. (1967) The use of tape-recorded programmes for craft training. Programmed Learning and Educational Technology, 4 (4), 196-201

ANDERSON, D.S. (1964) The person and environment in first year medicine in FRENCH, E.L. (Ed.) Melbourne Studies in Education 1961-62, 91-113, London, Cambridge University Press

ANDERSON, J. (1967) Testing clinical competence. British Journal of Medical Education, 1 (5), 345-347

ANDERSON, J., BUKITT, D., GEAL, M.A. and COCKER, P. (1968) How clinical students spend their time. British Journal of Medical Education, 2 (1), 4-10

APPLEBY, E.C. and POLAND, J. (1968) Some observations on the use of tape-recorded programmes in teaching veterinary pathology in Innovations and Experiments in University Teaching Methods, 30-34. University Teaching Methods Research Unit, London, London University Institute of Education

ARMSTRONG, R.H.R. and TAYLOR, J. (Eds.) (1970) Instructional Simulation Systems in Higher Education, Cambridge Monographs on Teaching Methods 2, Cambridge, Cambridge Institute of Education

ASH, P. and CARLTON, B.J. (1953) The value of note-taking during film learning. British Journal of Educational Psychology, 23, 121-125

ASHLEY, B. (1968) Group dynamics in human relations training. Case Conference, 15 (2)

AUSTRALIAN VICE-CHANCELLORS COMMITTEE (1963) Teaching Methods in Australian Universities. (Chairman: J.A. Passmore)

BAGG, D.A. (1968) The correlation of GCE A-level grades with university examinations in chemical engineering. British Journal of Educational Psychology, 38 (2), 194-197

BARCLAY, T.B. (1957) Effective reading. University of Edinburgh Gazette, 17, 22-30

BARNETT, S.A. (1958) An experiment with free discussion groups. Universities Quarterly, 12 (2), 175-180

BARRINGTON, H. (1965) A survey of instructional television researches. Educational Research, 8 (1), 8-25

BEARD, R.M. (1967a) An Inquiry into Small Group Discussion Methods in Three Disciplines, University Teaching Methods Research Unit, London, University of London Institute of Education

BEARD, R.M. (1967b) On evaluating the success of teaching. British Journal of Medical Education, 1 (4), 296-302

BEARD, R.M. (1969) A conspectus of research and development in Assessment of Undergraduate Performance, Universities Conference convened by the Committee of Vice-Chancellors and Principals and the Association of University Teachers, March 1969, London

BEARD, R.M. (1970) Teaching and Learning in Higher Education, Harmondsworth Penguin

BEARD, R.M., LEVY, P.M. and MADDOX, H. (1964) Academic performance at university. Educational Review, 16 (3), 163-174

BEARD, R.M., HEALEY, F.G. and HOLLOWAY, P.J. (1968) Objectives in Higher Education, London, Society for Research into Higher Education

BEARD, R.M. and POLE, K. (1971) The content and purpose of biochemistry examinations. British Journal of Medical Education, 51 (in press)

BENNET, W.A. (1968) The use of closed-circuit television for second language teaching in Innovations and Experiments in University Teaching Methods, University Teaching Methods Research Unit, London, University of London Institute of Education

BERKOWITZ, L., LEVY, B.I. and HARVEY, A.R. (1957) Effects of performance evaluations on group integration and motivation. Human Relations, 10, 195-208

BERNSTEIN, L., HEADLEE, R. and JACKSON, B. (1970) Changes in 'acceptance of others' resulting from a course in the physician-patient relationship. British Journal of Medical Education, 4 (1), 65-6

BESS, J.L. and BILORUSKY, J.L. (1970) Curriculum hypocrisies: studies of student initiated courses. Universities Quarterly, 24 (3), 291-309

BETTS, D.S. and WALTON, A.J. (1970) A lecture match or 'Anything you can do I can do better'. Physics Education, 5 (6), 321-325

BIRAN, L.A. (1966) A comparison of a scrambled and sequential presentation of a branching programme. Research Report on Programmed Learning, 9, National Council for Programmed Learning, University of Birmingham

BIRAN, L.A. and PICKERING, E. (1968) Unscrambling a herringbone: an experimental evaluation of branching programming. British Journal of Medical Education, 2, 213-9

BISHOP, A.T. and LEVY, L.B. (1968) Analysis of teaching behaviours. Education for Teaching, 76, 61-65

BLACK, P.J. (1968) University examinations. Physics Education, 3 (2), 93-99

BLACK, P.J., DYSON, N.A. and O'CONNOR, D.A. (1968) Group Studies. Physics Education, 3 (6), 289-293

BLAUG, M. (1968) Universities and Productivity, Universities Conference, March 1968

BLIGH, D.A. (1970) The case for a variety of teaching methods in each lesson. British Journal of Medical Education, 4 (3), 202-209

BLIGH, D.A. (1971) Teaching students in groups. (Typescript available from University Teaching Methods Unit, University of London Institute of Education)

BLIGH, D.A. (a) A pilot experiment to test the relative effectiveness of three kinds of teaching methods. Research in Librarianship (in press)

BLIGH, D.A. (b) Gropings for a Design of Objective Tests of the Effectiveness of Teaching Methods (unpublished)

BLIGH, D.A. (c) An Experiment to Compare the Teaching Effectiveness of a Tape-recorded Lecture at Three Speeds of Delivery (unpublished)

BLIGH, D.A. (d) An Experiment to Compare the Teaching Effectiveness of Lectures Delivered at Three Speeds (unpublished)

BLOOM, B.S. (Ed.) (1956) Taxonomy of Educational Objectives: I cognitive domain, New York, David McKay

BRITISH MEDICAL STUDENTS' ASSOCIATION (1965) Report on Medical Education: suggestions for the future, London, British Medical Association

BROADBENT, G. (1968) A plain man's guide to systematic design methods. RIBA Journal, May 1968, 223-227

BROCKBANK, J.P. (1969) New assessment techniques in use – the arts in Assessment of Undergraduate Performance, 19-22, Universities Conference convened by the Committee of Vice-Chancellors and Principals and the Association of University Teachers, Spring, 1969

BRYANT, K.H.J. and HOARE, D.E. (1970) First Year Chemistry in Australian Universities, The Australian Vice-Chancellors' Committee

BUCKLEY SHARP, M.D., HARRIS, F.T.C. TEPSON, J.B., SMITH, W.R.D. and WALKER, S. (1969) The evaluation of a programmed learning course. British Journal of Medical Education, 3 (2), 151-154

BURGE, R.E. (1968) Wider London B.Sc. Times Educational Supplement, 1st March 1968

BURKE, W.H. (1967) The new course and its development. Design Education, 2, 19-24, Hornsey College of Art

CARRÉ, C.G. (1969) Audio-tutorials as adjuncts to formal lecturing in biology teaching at the tertiary level. Journal of Biological Education, 3 (1), 57-64

CASTLE, W. and DAVIDSON, L. (1969) An evaluation of programmed instruction in a new medical faculty. British Journal of Medical Education, 3 (9), 359-361

CHALMERS, R.A. and STARK, J. (1968) Continuous assessment of practical work in the Scottish HNC course in chemistry. Education in Chemistry, 5 (4), 154-155

CHILD, D. (1970) Some aspects of study habits on higher education. International Journal of Educational Science, 4 (1), 11-20

CICIRELLI, V.G. (1969) University supervisors' creative ability and their appraisal of student teachers' classroom performance: an exploratory study. Journal of Educational Research, 62 (8), 375-381

COEKIN, J.A. (1969) Command of vocabulary among science and engineering students. Educational Research, 11 (2), 157-160

COEKIN, J.A. (1970) Teamwork with an industrial context in the second year electronics laboratory. International Journal of Engineering Education, 8 (2), 123-125

COGGLE, P.A. (1968) A programmed course in German for adult beginners in Innovations and Experiments in University Teaching, University Teaching Methods Research Unit, London, University of London Institute of Education

COLLARD, M., GRIFFITH, J., LIDDY, H., SHUK, V., SWINBURNE, E.S. (1969) The use of models and programmed learning in organic chemistry. Education in Chemistry, 6 (4), 130-132

COLLIER, K.G. (1966) An experiment in university teaching. Universities Quarterly, 20 (3), 336-348

COLLIER, K.G. (1969) Syndicate methods: further evidence and comments. Universities Quarterly, 23 (4), 431-436

COMMITTEE ON HIGHER EDUCATION (1963) Higher Education, London, Her Majesty's Stationery Office

CONNOR, D.J. (1968) Teaching engineering students by machine and text. Programmed Learning and Educational Technology, 5 (2), 129-135

CONNOR, D.V. (1967) A study of problem solving in physics. Australian Journal of Higher Education, 3 (1), 55-67

COOPER, B. and FOY, J.M. (1967) Evaluating the effectiveness of lectures. Universities Quarterly, 21 (2), 182-185

COOPER, B. and FOY, J.M. (1969) Students' study habits, attitudes and academic attainment. Universities Quarterly, 23 (2), 203-212

COOPER, C.L. (1968) A Study of the Role of the Staff Trainer in Human Relations Training Groups. Unpublished Ph.D. thesis, Department of Management, University of Leeds

COPE, E. (1969) Students and school practice. Education for Teaching, 25-35

COTTRELL, T.L. (1962) Effect of size of tutorial group on teaching efficiency. University of Edinburgh Gazette, 33, 20-21

COWAN, J., McCONNELL, S.G., and BOLTON, A. (1969-70) Learner Directed Group-Work for Large Classes, Department of Civil Engineering, Edinburgh, Heriot-Watt University

COX, R. (1967) Examinations and higher education. Universities Quarterly, 21 (3), 292-340

CRAIG, W.R. (1968) Experiment in television teaching and its reaction. International Journal of Electrical Engineering Education, 6 (2), 306-8

CROCKER, A.C. (1968) Predicting teacher success. Education for Teaching, 49-52

CROSSLEY, C.A. (1968) Tuition in the use of the library and of subject literature in the University of Bradford. Journal of Documentation, 24 (2), 91-97

CROWDER, N.A. (1958) Arithmetic of Computers, Edinburgh, Edinburgh University Press

CROXTON, P.C.L. and MARTIN, L.H. (1965) Away with notes (Programming in Higher Education). New Education, I, 25-27

CROXTON, P.C.L. and MARTIN, L.H. (1968) Progressive evaluation and the control of programmed classes in degree courses in TOBIN, M.J. (Ed.) Problems and Methods in Programmed Learning, Proceedings of the 1967 Association of Programmed Learning and the National Centre for Programmed Learning Birmingham Conference, 3, 83

CURETON, L. (1968) T-groups, Inter-groups in Teacher Training, University of Sussex, unpublished M.Phil. thesis

DAICHES, D. (1964) The Idea of a New University, London, Deutsch

DARKE, M. (1968) Teaching design methods. RIBA Journal, January 1968, 29-30

DAVEY, A.G. (1969) Leadership in relation to group achievement. Educational Research, 11 (3), 185-192

DAVIDSON, J.K. and THOMPSON, G.D.B. (1970) Closed-circuit television in teaching diagnostic radiology. British Journal of Medical Education, 4 (1), 23-28

DAVIES, A.E. (1968) The teaching capabilities of students. Bulletin of the British Psychological Society, 21 (71), 128

DAVIES, B.M. and MOWBRAY, R.M. (1968) Medical students' personality and academic achievement. British Journal of Medical Education, 2 (3), 195-199

DAVIES, G.N. (1967) Changing concepts in dental education. New Zealand Dental Journal, 63, 107-112

de CECCO, P. (1964) Class size and co-ordinated instruction. British Journal of Educational Psychology, 34, 65-74

de DOMBAL, F.T., HARTLEY, J.R. and SLEEMAN, D.H. (1969) A computer-assisted system for learning clinical diagnosis. Lancet, 1, 145-148

DEUTSCH, M. (1949) Experimental study of effects of co-operation and competition upon group process. Human Relations, 3, 199-231

DICK, W. (1963) Retention as a function of paired and individual use of programmed instruction, Journal of Programmed Instruction, 2 (3), 17-23

DICKINSON, L. (1970) The language laboratory in advanced teaching. English Language Teaching, 25 (1), 32-42

DOUGHTY, B.R. (1970) The use of a matrix in planning a teaching programme. British Journal of Medical Education, 4 (1), 19-22

DOUGLAS, A.M. (1970) An experiment in seminar methods. International Journal of Electrical Engineering Education, 8 (6), 519-523

DOWDESWELL, W.H. (1970) Inter-university biology teaching project. Journal of Biological Education, 4 (3), 197-203

DUCKWORTH, R. (1966) An evaluation of two methods of teaching the principles of pathology to dental students. British Dental Journal, 121 (5), 218-221

DUDLEY, H.A.F. (1970) Taxonomy of clinical educational objectives. British Journal of Medical Education, 4 (1), 13-18 du FEU, V.M. (1968) The language laboratory and minimal skills courses in Innovations and Experiments in University Teaching. Third Conference Report, University Teaching Methods Research Unit, London, University of London Institute of Education

DUNN, W.R. (1969) Programmed learning news: feedback devices in university lectures. New University, 3 (4), 21-22

EALING COURSE IN GERMAN (1968) London, Longmans

ECKERT, R.E. and NEALE, D.C. (1965) Teachers and teaching. Review of Educational Research, 35, 304-317

EDWARDS, C.H. (1967) Experience with an integrated first six months clinical training in Teaching for Efficient Learning, report of a conference held at the University of London Institute of Education, January 1967, University Teaching Methods Research Unit, London, University of London Institute of Education

EDWARDS, R. (1968) The training of educational researchers: a North American viewpoint. Bulletin of the British Psychological Society, 21 (1), 61-66

EGGLESTON, J.F. and KELLEY, P.J. (1970) The assessment of project work in A-level biology. Educational Research, 12 (3), 225-229

ELLEY, W.B. (1966) The role of errors in learning with feedback. British Journal of Educational Psychology, 31 (3), 296-300

ELLIOTT, A.G.P. (1958) An Experiment in Group Dynamics, mimeographed by Simon Eng., Ltd

ELTON, C.F. (1965) The effect of logic instruction on the Valentine Reasoning Test. British Journal of Educational Psychology, 35 (3), 339-341

ELTON, L.R.B. (1968) The assessment of students – a new approach. Universities Quarterly, 22 (3), 291-301

ELTON, L.R.B. (1968) Success and failure in university physics courses. Physics Education, 3 (6), 323-329

ELTON, L.R.B. (1970) Aims and objectives in the teaching of mathematics to non-mathematicians. Talk given at a conference on mathematics for students of other subjects, July, University of Lancaster

ELTON, L.R.B., HILLS, P.J. and O'CONNELL, S. (1970) Self-teaching situations in a university physics course. International Congress on the Education of Teachers of Physics in Secondary Schools, September, Eger, Hungary, 11-17

ENTWISTLE, N.J. and ENTWISTLE, D. (1970) The relationship between personality, study methods and academic performance. British Journal of Educational Psychology, 40 (2), 132-143

ENTWISTLE, N.J. and WILSON, J.D. (1970) Personality, study methods and academic performance. Universities Quarterly, 24 (2), 147-156

ERAUT, M. (1970) Course development: an approach to the improvement of teaching in higher education. Journal of Educational Technology, 1 (3), 195-206

ERSKINE, C.A. and O'MORCHOE, C.C.C. (1961) Research on teaching methods: its significance for the curriculum. Lancet, 23, 709-711

ERSKINE, C.A. and TOMKIN, A. (1963) Evaluation of the effect of the group discussion method in a complex teaching programme. Journal of Medical Education, 38, 1036-1042

FALK, B. (1966) The preparation and in-service training of university staff. Australian Journal of Higher Education, 2 (3), 200-206

FALK, B. (1967) The use of student evaluation. The Australian University, 5 (2), 109-121

FARRELL, W.H. (1965) Programmed learning in the Royal Canadian Air Force. Programmed Learning, 2 (3), 176-181

FLETCHER, S. and WATSON, A.A. (1968) Magnetic tape recording in the teaching of histopathology. British Journal of Medical Education, 2 (4), 283-292

FLOOD PAGE, C. (1970) The biggest stumbling block in university education. Universities Quarterly, 24 (3), 266-272

FLOOD PAGE, C. (1971) Technical Aids to Teaching in Higher Education, London, Society for Research into Higher Education

FOSTER, J. (1968) A note on the visibility of black-on-white and white-on-black photographic slides. British Psychological Society Bulletin, 21 (72)

FOULDS, K.W.H., HARLOW, R.G., JACKSON, D.F. and WHORLOW, R.W. (1969) Undergraduate physics projects at the University of Surrey. Physics Education, 4 (6), 344-345

FOY, J.M. (1969) A note on lecturer evaluation by students. Universities Quarterly, 23 (3), 345-348

FREYBERG, P.S. (1956) The effectiveness of note taking. Education for Teaching, February 1965, 17-24

FRY, E. (1963a) Teaching Faster Reading. London, Cambridge University Press

FRY, E. (1963b) Reading Faster. London, Cambridge University Press

FURNEAUX, W.D. (1962) The psychologist and the university. Universities Quarterly, 17, 33-47

GALLEGOS, A.M. (1968) Experimenter pacing and student pacing of programmed instruction. Journal of Educational Research, 61, 339-342

GALPARIN, P. Ya. (1957) An experimental study in the formation of mental actions in SIMON, B. (Ed.) Psychology in the Soviet Union, Stanford, California, Stanford University Press

GANE, C.P. (1969) Educational Technology v. the technology of education. The Royal Television Society Journal, 12 (5), 101-104

GANE, C.P., HORABIN, I.S. and LEWIS, B.N. (1966) The simplification and avoidance of instruction. Industrial Training International, July

GARBUTT, D. (1963) An investigation into students' understanding of some accountancy terms. The Vocational Aspect of Secondary and Further Education, 31 (15), 69-169

GARDINER, Q., BODDY, F.A. and TAYLOR, J. (1969) An orientation course for first-year medical students. British Journal of Medical Education, 3 (3), 199-202

GARDNER, M.J. (1969) An experiment in beer tasting. British Journal of Medical Education, 3 (3), 203-205

GAUVAIN, S. (1968) The use of student opinion in the quality control of teaching. British Journal of Medical Education, 2 (1), 55-62

GAUVAIN, S. (1970) Questionnaire Techniques in Course Evaluation, paper given to Symposium on Automation in Medical and other Higher Education, Multiple-Choice Questions and Research, June 1970

GAUVAIN, S., WOOD, C.H., WALFORD, J. and SCHILLING, R.S.F. (1965) Experiment in postgraduate education to evaluate teaching and examining techniques. Journal of Medical Education, 40 (1), 516-523

GIBB, G.O. (1968) Account of an experiment designed to test the effectiveness of a commentary superimposed over a televised classroom situation. Educational Television International, 2 (2)

GIBB, G.O. (1970) Presentation of video-tapes to college of education students. Education Television International, 4 (2)

GIBSON, J.N. (1970) Paper in a symposium on attitude measurement in explora- tory studies. Bulletin of the British Psychological Society, 23 (81), 323-324

GIDDAN, N.S., LOVELL, V.R., HARRISON, A.I. and HATTON, J.M. (1968) A scale to measure teacher-student interaction. Journal of Experimental Education, 36 (3), 52-58

GILL, N.M. (1970) Integrated studies in the B.Ed. course. Universities Quarterly, 24 (2), 195-200

GLYNN, E. (1965) Keys to chemistry (a personal effort in programming). New Education, I, 21-22

GOODHUE, D. (1969) Tape-recorded lectures with slide synchronization. A description of the method. Journal of Biological Education, 3 (4), 311-319

GOODLAD, S. (1970) Project work in developing countries: a British experiment in engineering education. International Journal of Electrical Engineering Education, 8 (2), 135-140

GRAVES, J. and GRAVES, V. (Eds.) (1963) Report on Conference on the Use of Tape in Medical Teaching at College of General Practitioners. Medical Recording Service and Sound Library, Royal College of General Practitioners

GRAVES, J. and GRAVES, V. (1965) Medical Sound Recording. London and New York, Focal Press

GRAVES, J. and GRAVES, V. (Eds.) (1967) Report on Second Conference on the Use of Audiotape in Medical Teaching. Medical Recording Service and Sound Library, Royal College of General Practitioners

GREENAWAY, H. (1971) Training of University Teachers: a survey of its provision in universities of the United Kingdom, London, Society for Research into Higher Education

GRUBB, R.E. (1968) Learner controlled statistics. Programmed Learning and Educational Technology, 5 (1), 38-42

GUILD, R.E. (1966) An experiment in modified programmed self-instruction. Journal of Dental Education, 30, 181-189

GUST, T. and SCHUMACHER, D. (1969) Handwriting speed of college students. Journal of Educational Research, 62 (5), 198-200

HALE, P.R. (1965) Using closed-circuit television. Cambridge Institute of Education Bulletin, 3 (1), 5-11

HALLWORTH, H.J. (1957) Group discussion in its relevance to teacher training. Educational Review, 10, 41-53

HALPIN, F.B. (1968) A predictive of failure in veterinary students: a method of selection for counselling. British Journal of Medical Education, 2 (3), 200-203

HAMMERSLEY, J.H. (1968) On the enfeeblement of mathematical skills by 'modern mathematics' and by similar soft track in schools and universities. Bulletin of the Institute of Mathematics and its Application, 4 (4), 1-22

HAMMOND, P. (1969) Are you happy with your syllabus? International Journal of Electrical Engineering Education, 7, 3-4

HANCOCK, A. and ROBINSON, J. (1966) Television and Social Work, London, National Institute of Adult Education

HARDEN, R.McG., WAYNE, Sir E. and DONALD, G. (1968) An audio-visual technique for medical teaching. Journal of Medical and Biological Illustration, 18 (1), 29-32

HARDEN, R.McG., DUNN, W.R., HOLROYD, C., LEVER, R., LINDSAY, A. and WILSON, G.M. (1969) An experiment involving substitution of tape/slide programmes for lectures. Lancet, May 3, 933-935

HARGREAVES, S. (1970) The Esso students' business game. The Technical Journal, 8 (5), 14-16

HARRINGTON, R.W. and KNOBLETT, J.A. (1968) Instructional closed-circuit television: a case study. Journal of Educational Research, 62 (1), 40-45

HARRISON, M.I. (1968) A computer-based learning system. Design Electronics, 5, 30-33

HARTLEY, J. (1968) Some factors affecting student performance in programmed learning. Programmed Learning and Educational Technology, 5 (3), 206-218

HARTLEY, J. and CAMERON, A. (1967) Some observations on the efficiency of lecturing. Educational Review, 20 (1), 30-37

HARTLEY, J.R. (1968) An experiment showing some student benefits against behavioural costs in using programmed learning. Programmed Learning and Educational Technology, 5 (3), 219

HAWKINS, J.D. (1969) A survey of student opinion on practical biochemistry in WILLS, E.D. (Ed.) Practical Biochemistry in the Medical Course, report of the Federal European Biochemical Society Summer School, April 1968

HAYES, D.M. (1964) Objective evaluation of a subjective teaching method: the student dissertation. Journal of Medical Education, 39, 1083-1089

HAYTHORN, W., COUCH, A., HAEFNER, D., LANGHAM, P. and LANNOR, F.C. (1956) The behaviour of authoritarian and egalitarian personalities in groups. Human Relations, 9, 57-74

HEALEY, F.G. (1967) Foreign Language Teaching in Universities, Manchester, Manchester University Press

HENSHAW, E.M., LANGDON, J. and HOLMAN, P. (1933) Manual Dexterity: Effects of Training, IHRB Report 67. London, Her Majesty's Stationery Office

HEWARD, C., MASH, V. and HEYWOOD, J. (1968) Student reaction to sandwich courses for the diploma in technology. Bulletin of Mechanical Engineering Education, 7, 253-268

HEYWOOD, J. (1969) Background Paper reference 10 in Assessment of Undergraduate Performance, Conference convened by the Committee of Vice-Chancellors and Principals and the Association of University Teachers, Spring 1969

HILL, B.J. (1969) The analysis of objectives for lecture courses in the physical sciences and engineering in Conference on Objectives in Higher Education, University Teaching Methods Research Unit, University of London Institute of Education

HILL, K.R. and SCHEUER, P.J. (1965) A rapid reading course. Royal Free Hospital Journal, 29, 23-25

HIRST, K. and BIGGS, N. (1969) Undergraduate projects in mathematics. Educational Studies in Mathematics, 1 (3), 252-261

HOARE, D.E. and INGLIS, G.R. (1965) Programmed learning in chemistry II: an experiment. Education in Chemistry, 2 (1), 32-35

HOARE, D.E. and REVANS, M.M. (1969) Measuring attainment of educational objectives in chemistry. Education in Chemistry, 6 (3), 78-80

HOLLAND, W.W., GARRAD, J., BENNETT, A.E. and RHODES, P. (1966) A clinical approach to the teaching of social medicine: an evaluation of an experimental method. Lancet, 1966 (1), 540-542

HOLLOWAY, P.J. (1964) A test of the use of a teaching aid for the instruction of undergraduate dental students in operative techniques. The Dental Practitioner, 14, 375-377

HOLLOWAY, P.J. (1966) The effect of lecture time on learning. British Journal of Educational Psychology, 31 (3), 255-258

HOLLOWAY, P.J., HARDWICK, J.L., MORRIS, J. and START, K.B. (1967) The validity of essay and viva-voce examining techniques. British Dental Journal, 123 (5), 227-232

HOLMES, E.L. (1970) Co-operative engineering education at the University of Waterloo. International Journal of Electrical Engineering Education, 8 (1), 3-10

HOLMES, P.G. (1969) An open-ended electrical machine laboratory for second-year undergraduates. International Journal of Electrical Engineering, 7 (3/4), 431-437

HOOLEY, T.M. and JONES, C. (1970) The influence of teacher attitude and student attitude in a programmed learning situation. Programmed Learning and Educational Technology, 7 (3), 189-193

HUDSON, L. (1966) Contrary Imaginations: A psychological study of the English schoolboy, London, Methuen

HUGHES, D.O. and MORGAN, E.D. (1970) A student exercise in X-ray crystallography. Education in Chemistry, 7 (2), 59-61

INHELDER, B. and PIAGET, J. (1958) The Growth of Logical Thinking, London, Routledge and Kegan Paul

INSTITUTE OF PHYSICS and the PHYSICAL SOCIETY (1960) The Postgraduate Training of Physicists in British Universities, Bristol Institute of Physics

ISHLER, R.E. (1967) The effectiveness of feedback as a means of changing student teachers' behaviour. Journal of Educational Research, 61 (3), 121-123

JAHODA, M. and THOMAS, L.F. (1966) The mechanics of learning. New Scientist, 30, 114-117

JAMES, D.W., JOHNSON, M.L.(now ABERCROMBIE, M.L.J.) and VENNING, P. (1956) Testing for learnt skill in observation and evaluation of evidence. Lancet, 1956 (2), 379-383

JAMES, P.E. (1970) A comparison of the efficiency of programmed video-tape and instruction booklet in learning to operate a desk calculator. Programmed Learning and Educational Technology, 7 (2), 134-139

JAMIESON, G.H. (1969) Learning by programmed and guided discovery methods at different age levels. Programmed Learning and Educational Technology, 6 (1) 26-30

JAMIESON G.H. (1970) The study of adult learning. Studies in Adult Education, 2 (1), 18-27

JAMIESON, G.H., JAMES, P.E. and LEYTHAM, G.W.H. (1969) Comparisons between teaching methods at the postgraduate level. Programmed Learning, 243-244

JEFFRIES, T.O. and LEECH, D.J. (1969) A student design contract. International Journal of Electrical Engineering Education, 7 (2), 182-191

JENKINS, D.E.P. (1968) The efficient use of laboratory time in the teaching of engineering in Innovations and Experiments in University Teaching Methods, University Teaching Methods Research Unit, London, University of London Institute of Education

JENKINS, M.I., SAUNDERS, E.H. and MACFARLANE SMITH, I. (1968) An experiment on the teaching of typewriting. The Vocational Aspect of Secondary and Further Education, 20 (45), 3-12

JEPSON, J. (1969) Some methods of teaching practical biochemistry in WILLS, E.D. (Ed.) Practical Biochemistry in the Medical Course, Federal European Biochemical Society Summer School, April 1968

JEVONS, F.R. (1970) Liberal studies in science – a successful experiment. Education in Chemistry, 7 (3), 98-99

JEWELL, B.R. (1970) Logistics of organizing a practical course. British Journal of Medical Education, 4 (3), 210-215

JONES, G. (1965) Organic research projects in an undergraduate course. Education in Chemistry, 2 (5), 238-240

JOHNSTON, J.O. and CALHOUN, J.A.P. (1969) The serial position effect in lecture material. Journal of Educational Research, 62 (6), 255-258

JONES, C.W. (1964) A Programmed Management Course: individual versus group administration. Department of Occupational Psychology, London

JONES, G.O. (1969) Physics in the new London B.Sc. degree. Physics Education, 4 (3), 143-150

JOYCE, C.R.B. and HUDSON, L. (1968) Student style and teacher style. British Journal of Medical Education, 2 (1), 28-31

JOYCE, C.R.B. and WEATHERALL, M. (1957) Controlled experiments in teaching. Lancet, 1957 (2), 402-407

JOYCE, C.R.B. and WEATHERALL, M. (1959) Effective use of teaching time. Lancet, 1959 (1), 568-571

KALLENBACH, W.W. and GALL, M.D. (1969) Microteaching v. conventional methods in training elementary intern teachers. Journal of Educational Research, 63 (3), 136-141

KATZ, F.M. and KATZ, C.N. (1968) Students' definition of the objectives of a university education. Australian Journal of Higher Education, 3 (2), 111-118

KAUFMAN, R.A. (1964) The systems approach to programming in OFIESH, G.D. and MEIERHENRY, W.C. (Eds.) Trends in Programmed Instruction, Papers from The National Society for Programmed Instruction and Department of Audio-Visual Instruction Conference, 1963

KENDALL, M. (1964) A Bibliography of Research into Higher Education, Research Unit for Student Problems, London, University of London.

KENSHOLE, G. (1968) A teaching experiment in a first-year university course. Physics Education, 3 (1), 49-50

KING, B.T. and IRVING, J.L. (1956) Comparison of the effectiveness of improvised versus non-improvised role-playing in producing opinion changes. Human Relations, 9, 177-186

KITCHEN, R.D. (1969) A study of teaching methods. Australian Journal of Higher Education, 3 (3), 218-225

KLEIN, J. (1961) Working with Groups, London, Hutchinson

KLEIN, J. (1965) The Study of Groups, London, Routledge and Kegan Paul

KLETZ, T.A. (1970) Putting knowledge to use. Education in Chemistry, 7 (6), 229

KRUMBOLTZ, J.D. (1964) The nature and importance of the required response in programmed instruction. American Journal of Educational Research, 1 (4), 203-209

KRUMBOLTZ, J.D. and WEISMAN, R.G. (1962) The effect of overt versus covert responding to programmed instruction on immediate and delayed retention. Journal of Educational Psychology, 53, 89-92

LEEDS, C.H. (1969) Predictive validity of the Minnesota Teacher Attitude Inventory. Journal of Educational Psychology, 20 (1), 51-56

LEITH, G.O.M. and BUCKLE, G.F. (1966) Mode of Response and Non-Specific Background Knowledge, National Centre for Research and Documentation of Programmed Learning, Birmingham, University of Birmingham

LEITH, G.O.M. and McHUGH, G.A.R. (1967) The place of theory in learning consecutive conceptual tasks. Educational Review, 19 (2), 110-117

LEITH, G.O.M. and WISDOM, B. (1970) An investigation of the effects of error making and personality on learning. Programmed Learning and Educational Technology, 7 (2), 120-126

LEWINSON, D. (1970) A self-testing device as an aid to learning. British Journal of Medical Education, 4 (2), 126-129

LEWIS, B.N. and PASK, G. (1964) The development of communication skills under adaptively controlled conditions. Programmed Learning, 1, 69-88

LEYTHAM, G.W.H. (1970) Learning and teaching, a review. British Journal of Educational Psychology, 40 (1), 90-93

LEYTON, E. (1966) The typical lecturer. New Society, 193, 12-13

LLOYD, D.H. (1968) A concept of improvement of learning response in the taught lesson. Visual Education, October, 23-25

McCARTHY, M.C. (1968) The Employment of Highly Specialized Graduates: a Comparative Study in the UK and the US, Department of Education and Science, Science Policy Studies, 3, London, Her Majesty's Stationery Office

McCARTHY, W.H. and GONELLA, J.S. (1967) The simulated patient management problem. British Journal of Medical Education, 1 (5), 348-352

McCLINTOCK, C.G. and TURNER, H.A. (1962) The impact of college upon political knowledge, participation and values. Human Relations, 15 (2), 163-176

MACFARLANE SMITH, I. (1968) An experimental study of the effect of television broadcasts on the G. course in Engineering Science 1 and 2. The Vocational Aspect of Secondary and Further Education, 20 (45), 78-85 and 20 (46), 89-100

McKEACHIE, W.J. (1966) Research in teaching : the gap between theory and practice in Improving College Teaching, American Council on Education

McKENZIE, N., ERAUT, M. and JONES, H.C. (1970) Teaching and Learning : and introduction to new methods and resources in higher education, UNESCO and the International Association of Universities

McKEVITT, O. (1967) The use of television recordings in university staff training. Australian Journal of Higher Education, 3 (1), 83-87

MacLAINE, A.G. (1963) An experiment with closed-circuit television at the University of Sydney. Australian Journal of Education, 7 (3), 157-164

MacLAINE, A.G. (1965) A programme for improving teaching and learning in Australian Universities. The Australian University, 3 (3), 235-266

McLEISH, J. (1966) Student retention of lecture material. A methodological study. Cambridge Institute of Education Bulletin, 3 (3), 2-11

McLEISH, J. (1968) The Lecture Method, Cambridge Monographs on Teaching Methods No. 1, Cambridge, Cambridge Institute of Education

McLEISH, J. (1970) Students' Attitudes and College Environments, Cambridge Monographs on Teaching Methods 3, Cambridge, Cambridge Institute of Education

MacMANAWAY, L.A. (1968) Using lecture scripts. Universities Quarterly, 22 (3), 327-336

MacMANAWAY, L.A. (1970) Teaching methods in higher education – innovation and research. Universities Quarterly, 24 (3), 321-329

McVEY, P.J. (1967) Evaluation of Four Lectures by means of Questionnaire. University of Surrey, Department of Electrical and Control Engineering, Report No. TR3

MADDOX, H. (1968) A descriptive study of teaching practice. Educational Review, 20 (3), 177-190

MAIER, N.R.F. and SOLEM, A.R. (1952) The contribution of a discussion leader to the quality of group thinking. Human Relations, 5 (3), 277-288

MALLESON, N. (1967) Medical students' study: time and place. British Journal of Medical Education, 1 (3), 169-177

MALLESON, N., PENFOLD, D. and SAWIRIS, M.Y. (1968) Medical students' study : the way they work. British Journal of Medical Education, 2, 11-19

MANN, P.H. and MILLS, G. (1961) A study of universities. Section III. Living and learning at Redbrick - I Academic conditions. Universities Quarterly, 16 (1), 19-24

MANNING, P.R., ABRAHAMSON, S. and DENNIS, D.A. (1968) Comparison of four teaching techniques : programmed text, textbook, lecture, demonstration, lecture workshop. Journal of Medical Education, 43 (3), 356-359

MARRIS, P. (1965) The Experience of Higher Education, London, Routledge and Kegan Paul

MARTIN, D.G. and LEWIS, J.C. (1968) Effective laboratory teaching. Bulletin of Mechanical Engineering Education, 7, 51-57

MILLS, D.G. (1966) The use of closed-circuit television in teaching geography and in training teachers of geography. Geography, 51 (3), 218-223

MOORE, D. (1967) Group teaching by programmed instruction. Programmed Learning and Educational Technology, 4 (1), 37-46

MOSCOW, D. (1968) The influence of interpersonal variables on the transfer of learning from the T-group to the job situation. Proceedings of the International Congress of Applied Psychology, Amsterdam, Swets and Zeitlinger

NATIONAL UNION OF STUDENTS (1969) Executive Report on Examinations, London, National Union of Students

NAY, M.A. and CROCKER, R.K. (1970) Science teaching and the affective attributes of scientists. Science Education, 54 (1), 59-67

NISBET, J. and WELSH, J. (1966) Predicting student performance. Universities Quarterly, 20 (4), 468-480

NOBLE, C.E. (1968) Annual Review of Psychology, 19, 203-250

O'CONNELL, S., WILSON, A.W. and ELTON, L.R.B. (1969) A pre-knowledge survey for university science students. Nature, 222, 526

ORR, W.G. (1968) Retention in comparing programmed and conventional instructional methods. Journal of Educational Research, 62 (1), 11-13

OWEN, S.G., HALL, R., ANDERSON, J. and SMART, G.A. (1965) A comparison of programmed learning instruction and lectures in the teaching of electrocardiography. Programmed learning, 2, 2-14

PEEL, E.A. (1968) Programmed thinking, in TOBIN, M.J. (Ed.) Problems and Methods in Programmed Learning, The Proceedings of the 1967 Association of Programmed Learning and the National Centre for Programmed Learning Birmingham Conference, 1

PERLSBERG, A. and RESH, M. (1967) Evaluation of the effectiveness of the overhead projector in teaching descriptive geometry and hydrology. Journal of Educational Research, 61 (1), 14-18

PERROT, E. and DUTHIE, J.H. (1969) University television in action : micro-teaching. University Television Newsletter, 7

PIAGET, J. (1926) Language and Thought of the Child, London, Routledge and Kegan Paul

PIKAS, A. (1969) Comparison between traditional and programmed learning as a function of passive performance and active application and time till application. Programmed Learning and Educational Technology, 6 (1), 20-25

PIPER, D.W. (1967) Strategies in course planning. Design Education 2, 16-18 Hornsey College of Art

POPPLETON, P.K. and AUSTWICK, K. (1964) A comparison of programmed learning and note-taking at two age levels. British Journal of Educational Psychology, 34 (1), 43-50

POULTON, E.C. (1961) British courses for adults on effective reading. British Journal of Educational Psychology, 31 (part II), 128-137

POWELL, J.P. (1966) Universities and University Education: A Select Bibliography, Slough, NFER

PROSSER, A.P. (1967) Oral reports on laboratory work in Teaching for Efficient Learning, report of a conference held at the University of London Institute of Education, January 1967. University Teaching Methods Research Unit, London, University of London Institute of Education

RAITT, J.G. (1968) Teacher training of graduate chemists. Chemistry in Britain, 4 (6), 242-244

RAYNER, S.A. (1966) The induction conference for new staff in the University of Queensland. Australian Journal of Higher Education, 2 (3), 189-199

REPIN, V. and ORLOV, R.S. (1967) The use of sleep and relaxation in the study of foreign languages. Australian Journal of Psychology, 19 (3), 203-207

REPORTS and PROCEEDINGS (1968) A course for university teachers, September 1967. Journal of Medical and Biological Illustration, 18 April 1968, 161

RESEARCH UNIT OF THE NATIONAL EXTENSION COLLEGE (1966a) University Intercommunication: The Nine Universities Research Project, Oxford, Pergamon Press

RESEARCH UNIT OF THE NATIONAL EXTENSION COLLEGE (1966b) A Survey of Audio-visual Activities in Universities and Colleges of Advanced Technology, Cambridge, National Extension College

RICHARDS, J.P.G. and WILSON, A.J.C. (1961) A-level and pass degree in physics. Universities Quarterly, 15 (4), 389-391

RICHARDSON, E. (1967) Group Study for Teachers, Students' Library of Education, London, Routledge and Kegan Paul

ROBERTSON, R.G. (1969) Teaching engineering by television. Chartered Mechanical Engineer, 16, 15-18

ROMISZOWSKI, A.J. (1967) A survey of the use of programmed learning in industry during 1966. Programmed Learning and Educational Technology, 4 (3), 210-215

ROSENBERG, E.H., FRIED, Y. and RABINOWITZ, G. (1970) A 'one-shot' group video-tape technique. British Journal of Medical Education, 4 (1), 32-36

ROTTGER, G.S. (1967) An experimental evaluation of group attractiveness as a determinant of conformity. Human Relations, 20 (3), 273-281

ROYAL COMMISSION ON MEDICAL EDUCATION 1965-66. The Todd Report (1968), London, Her Majesty's Stationery Office

SAUNDERS, M. et al. (1969) Report of the Commission on Teaching in Higher Education, London, National Union of Students

SCHONELL, F.J. et al. (1961a) Australian university experiment: problem and promise. Australian Journal of Science, 24 (1), 19-20

SCHONELL, F.J. et al. (1961b) University Teaching in Queensland: A report of conferences for demonstrators and lecturers,

SCHONELL, F.J., ROE, E. and MEDDLETON, I.G. (1962) Promise and Performance, University of Queensland Press

SCLARE, A.B. and THOMPSON, G.O.B. (1968) The use of closed-circuit television in teaching psychiatry to medical students. British Journal of Medical Education, 2 (3), 226-228

SENTER, R.J. et al. (1966) An Experimental Comparison of an Intrinsically Programmed Text and a Narrative Text, Final Report No.AMRL-TR-65-227. Aero-Space Medical Research Laboratories, Wright Patterson AFB, Ohio

SEYMOUR, W.D. (1937) An experiment showing the superiority of a light coloured 'blackboard'. British Journal of Educational Psychology, 7, 259-268

SEYMOUR, W.D. (1966) Industrial Skills, London, Pitman

SHERWIN, E. and CHILD, D. (1970) Predicting the performance of under-graduate chemists. Education in Chemistry, 7 (4), 156-158

SHOUKSMITH, G. (1969) Experimental psychology in large introductory classes. Bulletin of the British Psychological Society, 22 (77), 293-296

SIME, M. and BOYCE, G. (1969) Overt responses, knowledge and results of learning. Programmed Learning and Educational Technology, 6 (1), 12-19

SIMPSON, R.H. (1965) The use of self-evaluation procedures by lecturers in educational psychology. Educational Review, 18 (1), 25-33

SLAVINA, L.S. (1957) Specific features of the intellectual work of unsuccessful pupils in SIMON, B. (Ed.) Psychology in the Soviet Union, Stanford, California, Stanford University Press

SMITH, G. and WYLLIE, J.H. (1965) Use of closed-circuit television in teaching surgery to medical students. British Medical Journal, 1965 (2), 99-101

SMITH, G., WYLLIE, J.H., FORTE, A.V. and CARADIS, D.T. (1966) Further studies of the use of closed-circuit television in teaching surgery to undergraduate students. British Journal of Medical Education, 1, 40-42

SMITH, P.B. (1964) Attitude changes associated with training in human relations. British Journal of Sociology and Clinical Psychology, 2, 104-112

SMITH, P.B. (1969a) Improving Skills in Working with People : the T-group, Training Information Paper 4, London, Her Majesty's Stationery Office

SMITH, P.B. (1969b) T-group climate, trainer style and some tests of learning in MILES, M.B. and HJELHOLT, G. (Eds.) Development, National Training Laboratories

SMITH, P.B. and POLLACK, H.B. (1968) The participant's learning style as a correlate of T-group learning. Proceedings of the International Conference of Applied Psychology, Amsterdam, Swets and Zeitlinger

SMITHERS, A. (1970a) Some factors in lecturing. Educational Review, 22 (2) 141-150

SMITHERS, A. (1970b) Open-mindedness and the university curriculum. Journal of Curriculum Studies, 2 (1), 73-77

SMITHERS, A. (1970c) What do students expect of lectures? Universities Quarterly, 330-336

SMITHERS, A.G. and HAMBLER, D.J. (1969) The bearing of the sandwich course on university education of biologists. Journal of Biological Education, 3 (3), 209-220

SPECIAL CORRESPONDENT (1966a) Necropsy demonstrations relayed by television. British Medical Journal, 1966 (1), 478

SPECIAL CORRESPONDENT (1966b) Closed-circuit television between medical schools. British Medical Journal, 1966 (1), 1476-1477

SPROTT, W.J.H. (1958) Human Groups, Harmondsworth, Penguin

STAVERT, G.S. (1969) Programmed learning in action. Bacie Journal, 23 (1), 16-20

STAVERT, G.S. and WINGATE, T.H. (1966) Nelson's Navy needed none but ...! Tutor Age, 17, 2-7

STEINBERG, H. and LEWIS, H.E. (1951) An experiment on the teaching value of a scientific film. British Medical Journal, 1951 (2), 465-471

STUEBNER, E.A. and JOHNSON, R.P. (1969) A hospital clerkship programme for dental students : an exploratory study. Journal of Dental Education, 33 (2), 224-229

STEWART-TULL, D.E.S. (1970) The setting and marking of microbiology examinations. Journal of Biological Education, 4 (1), 25-42

STONES, E. (1966) The effects of different conditions of working on student performance and attitudes. Programmed Learning, 3 (3), 135-145

STONES, E. (1966) An Experiment in the Use of Programming Technique in the Training of Student Teachers, University of Nottingham Institute of Education, Educational Paper 7

STONES, E. (1967) Strategies and tactics in programmed instruction in TOBIN M.J. (Ed.) Problems and Methods in Programmed Learning, the proceedings of the 1967 Association of Programmed Learning and National Centre for Programmed Learning Birmingham Conference, 62

STONES, E. (1968) An Experiment in the Use of Programmed Learning in a University with an Examination of Student Activities and the Place of Seminar Discussion in TOBIN, M.J. (Ed.), Problems and Methods in Programmed Learning. The Proceedings of the 1967 Association of Programmed Learning and National Centre for Programmed Learning Birmingham Conference

STONES, E. (1969) Students' attitudes to the size of teaching groups. Educational Review, 21 (2), 98-108

STONES, E. and ANDERSON, D. (1970) Objectives and the Teaching of Educational Psychology, Birmingham University School of Education

STRETTON, T.B., HALL, R. and OWEN, S.G. (1967) Programmed learning in medical education. Comparison of teaching machine and programmed textbook. British Journal of Medical Education, 1 (3), 165-168

STUDENTS' SOCIETY COMMITTEE OF ROYAL DENTAL HOSPITAL SCHOOL OF DENTAL SURGERY (1966) Report on opinion poll on the lecture courses. Supplement to Extract, 33, Part I

SWANN REPORT (1968) The flow into employment of scientists, engineers and technologists. Committee on Manpower Resources for Science and Technology, CMND 3760, London, Her Majesty's Stationery Office

TANSEY, P.J. (1969) Simulation and teacher education. Education for Teaching, 79, 63-68

TAPLIN, G. (1969) The Cosford Cube: a simplified form of student feedback. Industrial Training International, 4 (5), 218-219

TAYLOR, J.L. and CARTER, K.R. (1967) Instructional simulation of urban development: a preliminary report. Town Planning Institute Journal, 53 (10), 443-447

TAYLOR, J.L. and MADDISON, R.N. (1967) A land use gaming simulation. SCUPAS Bulletin 4, Proceedings of 2nd Salzburg conference in urban planning and development, 18-22 May 1967

TAYLOR, R.G. and HANSON, G.R. (1969) Pre-college mathematics workshop and freshman achievement. Journal of Educational Research, 64 (3), 157-160

TEATHER, D.C.B. (1968) Programmed learning in biology. Journal of Biological Education, 2, 119-135

THODAY, D. (1957) How undergraduates work. Universities Quarterly, 11 (2), 172-181

THORNDIKE, E.L. (1913) The Psychology of Learning, New York, Teachers College, Columbia University

TOBIN, M.J. (1968) Technical education and industrial training. Educational Technology, 10 (11), 442-444

TRENAMAN, J.M. (1967) Communication and Comprehension, London, Longmans

TROWN, A. (1970) Some evidence on the interaction between teaching strategy and personality. British Journal of Educational Psychology, 40 (2), 209-211

TUBBS, M.R. (1968) Seminars in experimental physics. Physics Education, 3 (4), 189-192

TUCKMAN, J. and LORGE, I. (1962) Individual ability as a determinant of group superiority. Human Relations, 15 (1), 45-57

UNIVERSITY GRANTS COMMITTEE (1964) Report of the Committee on University Teaching Methods (Chairman: Sir E. Hale) London, Her Majesty's Stationery Office

UNIVERSITY GRANTS COMMITTEE, DEPARTMENT OF EDUCATION AND SCIENCE and SCOTTISH EDUCATION DEPARTMENT (1965) Report of the Committee on Audio-Visual Aids in Higher Scientific Education (Chairman: Brynmor Jones) London, Her Majesty's Stationery Office

UNIVERSITY TEACHING METHODS RESEARCH UNIT (1966) Teaching Methods in University Departments of Science and Medicine, Report of the first conference organized by the Unit, January 1966, London (out of print) University of London Institute of Education

UNIVERSITY TEACHING METHODS RESEARCH UNIT (1967) Teaching for Efficient Learning, Report of the second conference organized by the Unit, January 1967, London, University of London Institute of Education

UNIVERSITY TEACHING METHODS RESEARCH UNIT (1968) Innovations and Experiments in University Teaching Methods, Report of the third conference organized by the Unit, April 1968, London, University of London Institute of Education

UNWIN, D. (1966) An 'organizational' explanation for certain retention and correlation factors in a comparison between two teaching methods. Programmed Learning, 3, 1

UREN, O. (1968) The Use of Texts in Language Skill Development: some problems, Report of the third conference organized by the Unit, April 1968, University Teaching Methods Research Unit, London, University of London Institute of Education

VALVERDI, H.H. and MORGAN, R.L. (1970) Influence of student achievement of redundancy in self-instructional materials. Programmed Learning and Educational Technology, 7 (3), 194-199

VAN der WILL (1968) The language laboratory in advanced language teaching: gimmick or challenge in Innovations and Experiments in University Teaching Methods, 57-63, Report of the third conference organized by the Unit, April 1968, London, University Teaching Methods Research Unit, London, University of London Institute of Education

VERNON, P.E. (1946) An experiment on the value of the film and film-strip in the instruction of adults. British Journal of Educational Psychology, 16, 149-162

VERNON, M.D. (1953) Perception and understanding of instructional television programmes. British Journal of Psychology, 44, 116-126

WAKEFORD, J. (1968) The Teaching Methods and Techniques in Sociology, paper read at British Sociological Association Teachers' Section Conference, Bedford College, January 1968

WAKEFORD, J. (1968) The Strategy of Social Inquiry, London, Macmillan

WALKLEY, G.H. (1969) Increasing the efficiency of the university examination system. Education in Chemistry, 6 (3), 88-94

WALLIS, D., DUNCAN, K.D. and KNIGHT, M.A.G. (1966) The Halton experiment and the Melksham experiment in Programmed Instruction in the British Armed Forces, London, Her Majesty's Stationery Office

WALTON, H.J. and DREWERY, J. (1964) Teaching psychiatry to undergraduate medical students. Journal of Medical Education, 29 (6), 545-552

WALTON, H.J. and DREWERY, J. (1966) Psychiatrists as teachers in medical schools. British Journal of Psychiatry, 112, 839-846

WALTON, H.J. and DREWERY, J. (1967) The objective examination in the evaluation of medical students. British Journal of Medical Education, 1 (4), 255-264

WATSON, N. (1964) A method of assessing the studio work of architecture students. RIBA Journal, 71, 358-360

WELSER, J.R. (1970) Silent loop films in the teaching of anatomy. British Journal of Medical Education, 4 (2), 120-125

WHITELAND, J.W.R. (1966) The selection of research students. Universities Quarterly, 21 (1), 44-47

WILLIAMS, E.R. and WOODING, E.R. (1967) Planning a lecture course with the aid of network analysis. Physics Education, 2 (4), 202-206

WILLIAMS, E.R. and WOODING, E.R. (1968) The postgraduate education of physicists. Physics Education, 3 (3), 152-156

WILLIAMS, J.P. (1963) Comparison of several modes in a review programme. Journal of Educational Psychology, 54, 253-260

WILLS, E.D. (Ed.) (1969) Practical Biochemistry in the Medical Course: A report of the Federal European Biochemical Society Summer School, April 1968

WILSON, J.F. (1966) A survey of legal education in the UK. The Journal of the Society of Public Teachers of Law, 9 (1), 1-44

WISPE, L.G. (1951) Evaluating section teaching methods in the introductory course. Journal of Educational Research, 45, 161-186

WOOD, C.C. and HEDLEY, R.L. (1968) Student reaction to VTR in simulated classroom conditions. Canadian Educational Research Digest, 8 (1), 46-59

WOOD, D.N. (1969) Library education for scientists and engineers. Bulletin of Mechanical Engineering Education, 8 (1), 1-9

WOODING, E.R. (1968) Third-year laboratory projects in physics. Innovations and Experiments in University Teaching Methods, 75-80, University Teaching Methods Research Unit, London, London Institute of Education

WOODFORD, G.A. (1969) Teacher influence in a college of education. Educational Research, 11 (2), 148-152

WOODS, C.S. and NORTHCOTT, P.H. (1970) An Audio-visual Innovation in Undergraduate Teaching: a Progress Report, Australian Geography Teachers Association, June

WRAGG, E.C. (1970) Interaction analysis as a feedback system for student teachers. Education for Teaching, Spring, 38-47

WRIGHT, E.A. (1968) A research project for clinical medical students in Innovations and Experiments in University Teaching Methods, 70-75, University Teaching Methods Research Unit, London, London Institute of Education.

WRIGHT, P. (1967) The use of questions in programmed learning. Programmed Learning and Educational Technology, 4 (2), 103-107

WRIGHT, P. (1968) Reading to learn. Chemistry in Britain, 4 (10), 445-450

INDEX